interest in the last two decades of the 1800's; (4) a period in which the United States attempted to intervene directly in Latin-American affairs; (5) the good neighbor period; and (6), contemporaneously, a period in which many crosscurrents are visible.

Finally, Dr. Perkins approaches the subject of economics—which is at the same time one of the strongest ties between Latin America and the United States and one of the broadest areas of misunderstanding.

The question of "economic imperialism" has been argued at length, but Dr. Perkins points out that the crux of the answer is this: "It lies with the state which receives foreign capital to regulate the conditions under which it operates, and to see that the social interest of the total community is well served and protected."

"These essays," says Charles C. Griffin of the Department of History at Harvard, "fill a very useful purpose in that they provide brief, interesting, and authoritative surveys of important subjects. They should be useful both to college students and to the general public."

THE AUTHOR

DEXTER PERKINS is Professor Emeritus of Cornell University and the University of Rochester. Included among his many volumes about American relations with Latin America are *Hands Off: The History of the Monroe Doctrine, The Evolution of American Foreign Policy, The United States and the Caribbean,* and *The American Approach to Foreign Policy.*

DAVIS WASHINGTON MITCHELL LECTURES
TULANE UNIVERSITY

Previously published in this series:

THE AMERICAN UNIVERSITY IN THE TWENTIETH
CENTURY
by William Clyde DeVane

SCIENCE AND LIBERAL EDUCATION
by Bentley Glass

THE UNITED STATES
AND LATIN AMERICA

DEXTER PERKINS

THE UNITED STATES
AND
LATIN AMERICA

LOUISIANA STATE UNIVERSITY PRESS
BATON ROUGE

Other Books by Dexter Perkins

The Monroe Doctrine, 1823–1826 (*1927*)
The Monroe Doctrine, 1826–1867 (*1933*)
John Quincy Adams as Secretary of State (*1938*)
The Monroe Doctrine, 1867–1907 (*1938*)
Hands Off: The History of the Monroe Doctrine (*1941*)
America and the Two Wars (*1944*)
The United States and the Caribbean (*1947*)
The Evolution of American Foreign Policy (*1948*)
The American Approach to Foreign Policy (*1952*)
Charles Evans Hughes and American
Democratic Statesmanship (*1956*)

© 1961
Louisiana State University Press
Library of Congress Catalogue Card Number: 61–7544
Manufactured in the United States of America by
J. H. Furst Company, Baltimore, Maryland

FOREWORD

THE DAVIS WASHINGTON MITCHELL FUND was established in 1954 at Tulane University to provide for a series of lectures dealing with subjects which are " stimulative of independent thought and gracious living, and which may increase devotion to the public good." Characteristic of the man in whose honor the Davis Washington Mitchell Lectures were named, these goals were the only restrictions placed on the Fund by the late Mrs. Ida Mitchell Looney when she established it in the memory of her grandfather.

These Lectures were the culmination of a lifetime of gifts and work in the fields of patriotic societies, Southern history, and higher education, on the part of Mrs. Looney. Her death on March 1, 1958, came only two weeks before the second series of Lectures were presented.

Previous lecturers who have appeared at Tulane University through this endowment are William Clyde DeVane, Sanford Professor of English at Yale University and Dean of Yale College, and Bentley Glass, Professor of Biology at The Johns Hopkins University.

PREFACE

It was a great pleasure for me to give at Tulane University, so distinguished an institution in its interests in Latin-American affairs, the three lectures which follow in essay form. Today, more than ever before, we are confronted with serious problems in relation to the undeveloped countries of the world. The central problem is to what degree and in what manner we can retain their good will at a time when our economy is so flourishing and when in other parts of the world there exists an impatient desire to move forward. The highest standards will be demanded of us in meeting this challenge. I hope that what I have had to say in this little book will provide some illumination on the subject.

Since the delivery of the lectures last winter, events in Cuba have moved rapidly toward the close association of that state with the Soviet Union. The observations made in my second chapter on the political developments of Latin America may, therefore, seem overoptimistic. I am, however, willing to stand by them, from the long-term point of view.

Rochester, N. Y., 1960   Dexter Perkins

ix

CONTENTS

Foreword vii

Preface ix

Latin America and National Security . . . 3

Latin-American Political Relations
    with the United States 45

Latin-American Economic Relations
    with the United States 87

xi

THE UNITED STATES
AND LATIN AMERICA

LATIN AMERICA
AND NATIONAL SECURITY

As in most human activities, there are fashions in historical study. In American history over the last sixty years the study of politics has been followed by a stress on economic factors, then on social factors, then on intellectual. In the field of international affairs there have been similar changes in emphasis. Just now, there seems to be an enormous vogue with regard to what is described as non-Western civilization. It is not hard to understand the reasons for this fashion. The dramatic events in the Far East, the hardly less arresting developments in the area now known as the Middle East, have created a fresh, wide, and legitimate interest in this area. But sometimes this interest seems disproportionate.

Let us look at the matter from the standpoint of the secular struggle between the Communist and the non-Communist world. We have every reason to believe that this struggle will last for some time, and every interest in seeing that the values we believe in are fortified and perpetuated. Viewing the various areas in which the competition of systems is likely to take

3

place, in which are we most likely to exert the most effective influence? In which is the general situation more favorable to us? Western Europe stands first, by all odds, I hope we shall all agree. But after that are not our chances best in Latin America? In Latin America there is no vexing and explosive question of recent colonialism. The Latin Americans have been free for more than a century and a quarter. There, the various republics, even those with an infusion of Indian blood, feel themselves to be part of the civilization of the West. There, powerful economic ties exist, binding the nations of the South to the United States. To say this is not to say that there are no problems, no sources of tension or of rivalry. It is not to discount the many difficulties that lie in our path. It is truly to suggest that the chances of a fruitful relationship are far better than in Asia or Africa, or the Middle East. Because this is so, an historical review of our Latin-American policy may prove to be of special interest.

There is, however, one respect in which, it must be conceded, the states of the Western hemisphere are *less* important than is commonly assumed. We must, of course, seek to take the balanced view, and if we do so, we shall be forced to concede that from the standpoint of national security, construed in terms of direct physical peril, the contemporary world presents a picture in which Latin America is of secondary importance. I would go further and say that it has never been of first importance.

I approach the question of the relationship of the national security to Latin America with the more gusto because it seems to me that there are a good many superstitions and shibboleths to be demolished in the course of any historical analysis of the problem. The history of our Latin-American diplomacy is filled with examples of the manner in which vague generalizations capture the public mind and have their effect upon policy.

We shall, then, naturally begin with the famous pronouncement of December 2, 1823, which is known to history as the Monroe Doctrine. Old stuff! I can imagine my readers thinking. Is this man, you are asking, going to rehash what he put into four volumes, the last of which appeared twenty years ago? Let me reassure you. I have something new to say on that subject. The exciting thing about history is that the longer you brood upon the facts, the more likely you are to extract a new meaning from them.

Let us look once more at the language of the President in his famous message. "We owe it to candor," he declared, " and to the amicable relations existing between the United States and those powers [i. e., the

European powers], to declare that we should consider any attempt on their part to extend their system to any portion of this hemisphere as dangerous to our peace and safety." There is certainly nothing equivocal about that. The principle of national security is invoked as clearly as words can invoke it. But as we think the matter over, why?

A moment's reflection on the geography of the New World suggests that Monroe was indulging in fantasy. From Buenos Aires to New York by sea (and there was no other way to get from one city to the other in 1823) is 5,871 miles. From Rio de Janeiro to New York is 4,770 miles. From Valparaiso to New York is 4,634 miles. From Puntas Arenas in southern Chile to New York is 5,960 miles. Can it, then, be seriously contended that the establishment in such countries of regimes different in form from that of the United States would seriously threaten this country? In what sense were Chile, or Argentina, or Brazil, dangerous to our peace and safety under *any* government? Precisely what was the peril to be feared? Let us suppose (most improbably) that these regions, whose independence had been established, were to be reconquered by Spain or, in the case of Brazil, by Portugal. Was it likely, was it even possible, that the regimes thus established would be able to embark on ambitious enterprises that imperiled the national interests of the United States?

But what did Monroe mean when he spoke of extending the European system to the New World? Did he mean that monarchy, in itself, was dangerous? One can hardly believe so, for the United States had already recognized the monarchist government of Iturbide in Mexico and was shortly to recognize the royalist government of Brazil. Did he mean that monarchy under European auspices was dangerous? Probably so. But was he right? Let us suppose, for the sake of argument, that the European powers had been able to bring about the establishment of kingdoms in Latin America, under younger members of the House of Bourbon. Would this have been substantially different from the situation in Brazil? In what sense would this have constituted a threat to the United States? To what degree is the internal organization of any other state a matter of legitimate concern to the authorities in Washington? The latter question is a particularly complex one, and we shall examine it in more detail in my second essay. But I think we can agree here that, as a mere historical matter, the United States has recognized governments of all sorts in the last 138 years, and that what matters most is not the internal form, but the external purposes of the regimes in question.

But what is the true relationship of the Monroe message to the question of national security? Have no security considerations been involved in the long loyalty of the American people to the doctrines of 1823? In answering this question, there are two matters that ought to be examined. The first is the degree to which there existed a threat to American security interests in the New World. The second is as to how far such a threat was *felt* to exist and how far this feeling actually affected policy.

No legend is more persistent than the legend that the countries of the New World were in grave danger from Europe and that the Monroe Doctrine protected them from being overrun by the wicked nations of the Old World. A corollary to this legend is that, though the United States was unable effectively to prevent such action, any hostile move was prevented by the British domination of the seas. Neither of these things happens to be true.

I shall not review the analysis which I made many years ago, and in which I showed that there was no intention to reconquer the colonies in 1823. But in the long period from the enunciation of the Doctrine to the end of the century, from what continental European power could any assault upon the liberties of the new be assumed to come? There was not until 1871 any unified Germany, and German naval power was not developed until the end of the century. The Austrian monarchy was oriented toward the East, and had plenty of internal problems as well. The great Russian state was preoccupied either with the Slav nations to the south or with expansion eastward. Italy, never a state of the first rank, was for a large part of the period a geographical expression. For much of the period the only power that could, by virtue of its naval power, play an expansionist role in the New World was France.

Let us look, then, at the actual development of French policy. That the French had territorial ambitions in the New World, in the literal sense, is not at all likely. In 1838, and again in 1847–48 (the second time in concert with Great Britain), the French instituted a blockade against the extremely unsavory dictator who ruled the Argentine Republic, Juan Manuel de Rosas. Undoubtedly, they would have been delighted if they could have overthrown him. But there is no evidence whatever that what was contemplated was the establishment of any territorial base on the soil of the New World, and, indeed, it would have been quite uncharacteristic of the government of the July monarchy, of its sovereign, and of its chief ministers, if such a thing had been contemplated.

The situation under Louis Napoleon was different. The establishment of the Austrian Archduke Maximilian upon a shaky throne in Mexico was an enterprise which could hardly fail to arouse American susceptibilities. One of the reasons why it failed was the attitude of the United States. But mature reflection on the matter has led me to the conviction that it was foredoomed in any case. It was profoundly unpopular in France itself; it imposed on the French people heavy financial burdens, which were widely resented; more important than either of these factors, it met with the determined resistance of the Mexican themselves. What it illustrates is that any attempt to impose an alien regime on an American people would, in the nature of the case, be met with widespread opposition on the part of the people concerned. Moreover, it stands virtually alone as an example of French ambition in the New World.

Indeed, the government of the Third Republic, which was established in 1871, never nourished any ambitions to extend its rule in Latin America. It embarked upon a policy of expansion in North Africa, beginning with the establishment of a protectorate over Tunis in 1883, and extending its influence over Morocco; it established itself in Annam, in Tonkin, in Madagascar, in large areas of Africa; and its preoccupation with these enterprises suggests that, in the nature of the case, European colonial ambition would be far more likely to concern itself with areas where it had the best chance of succeeding, rather than with crossing thousands of miles of ocean to attempt to conquer states which had attained a very substantial measure of coherence by the third quarter of the nineteenth century.

Let me emphasize those words " a very substantial measure of coherence." It is sometimes the fashion to dwell upon the instability of Latin-American regimes, and to picture the whole of the Latin-American world as a prey to constant convulsion and change, offering a fertile field to intervention by an ambitious outside power. But the facts do not bear out this view. It is certainly true that states like the Dominican Republic and the Republic of Haiti were for a long time vexed by constant revolutions, alternating with periods of dictatorial rule, though it is fair to say of the Dominican Republic that, disordered as it often was, it made things hot for the Spaniards when they tried to re-establish their control there in 1861–65. But we must not judge by the worst examples. The big three—Argentina, Brazil, and Chile—had embarked upon a long period of orderly government by the second half of the century, to which the republican revolution in Brazil offers no very great exception. Mexico was under strong dictatorial rule from 1878 to 1910. There was less to be said in praise of the course of events in Central America, or in some of the other states of South America. But no statesman in his senses would have failed to realize that these states, whatever their domestic discords, would be troublesome customers if any attempt were made to subject them to foreign rule. This does not mean that European governments were averse to spanking these various regimes when they misbehaved. But this was a very different thing from attempting to subvert them. And indeed, down to the end of the century, spanking them was recognized as a legitimate pastime by the government of the United States itself.

But what about Germany? What about the Germany of the Kaiser, in particular, and what about the situation that existed before the First World War? In the thirty years after the establishment of the Empire, German interest in Latin America was growing. Toward the turn of the century there can be little doubt that certain elements in the Reich were interested in extending German power, especially German naval power, to the New World. The German Admiralty, in particular, had an itch for naval bases in the American hemisphere. The Virgin Islands, Curacao, St. Eustatius, Dutch Guiana, southern Brazil, all came within the range of Admiral Alfred von Tirpitz' vision. Pan-German elements looked with an acquisitive eye on the last-named of these areas, where there were many German settlers. But it would be a mistake to take the views of naval officers or of superheated German patriots as the views of the German government itself. On occasion, the naval office was actually slapped down; and more than one direct assurance was given to the American government that Germany harbored no territorial ambitions in Latin America.

There is, of course, the famous Venezuela episode of 1902–1903. This is the occasion when the Germans and the British joined in a blockade of the coast of the Venezuelan republic with a view to inflicting chastisement on the highly unsavory dictator, Cipriano Castro, who was then in power. The events of this era derive their special interest from the highly colored narrative with regard to the matter later circulated by President Theodore Roosevelt, in which he pictured himself as staving off by a firm policy, indeed by an ultimatum, the sinister designs of the Kaiser and his minions. " I became convinced," wrote Roosevelt, " that Germany intended to seize some Venezuelan harbor and turn it into a strongly fortified place of arms, on the model of Kiauchau, with a view to exercising some degree of control over the future Isthmian Canal, and over South American affairs generally." This famous account has been the subject of much discussion by historians.

Rather recently, it has been examined by the late Professor Howard Beale of the University of Wisconsin. Professor Beale was disposed to see at least some truth in the Roosevelt narrative. I can only say that I must dissent strongly. Professor Beale wrote without benefit of the German or British archives for the period in question. It is an interesting fact that an examination of those archives (and such an examination I made in 1935) does not give the slightest substantiation to the Roosevelt story. There is not a word in any of the documents that suggests Germany had the slightest ulterior designs in the blockade of Venezuela. It seems almost incredible that such should have been the case if an nefarious plot was under way. There are other facts which support the same conclusion. Germany, in her correspondence with Great Britain, had explicitly rejected the idea of the permanent occupation of Venezuelan territory before beginning the blockade. Why should she have associated the British government with her own activities if she intended some kind of conquest? And why should she have accepted the idea of arbitration, at least in principle, a few days after instituting the blockade if she were bent on the permanent occupation of territory? After the fullest reconsideration of the problem, I believe that it can be stated categorically that there was no ulterior purpose behind the naval operations of 1902.

But we must not go beyond the facts in the desire for a tidy generalization. There is at least one incident which suggests that the Germans were not entirely free of a desire to intermeddle in American affairs in a way that might have involved—at long range—security consideration. In 1914, just before the outbreak of the First World War, the German chargé suggested that Germany must have a hand in any customs control of the then extremely turbulent and disorganized Republic of Haiti. He did not suggest exclusive control; but an arrangement of this kind might easily have led to trouble, and it met with a prompt response from the American State Department. It is a slender basis, however, on which to rest the case that the republics of the New World were in deadly danger from European ambition.

So much for the thesis that the Monroe Doctrine saved the Latin-American republics from extinction, or conquest. Let us look now at the companion thesis that these republics owe their safety to the British navy. It is not difficult to see why this assumption became popular. At a time when close relations with Britain were extremely important to the United States, as in the years leading up to World War II, it was useful to put forward the view that we owed a debt to Britain as a result of her benevolent attitude towards the New World. This proposition was given widespread publicity by one of the most distinguished of American publicists, Walter Lippmann. It does not, however, correspond with reality.

As a matter of fact, the only power that extended its control over New World territory in the nineteenth century was Great Britain. The British seized the Falkland Islands in 1833; they extended their jurisdiction in what is now British Honduras, annexed the Bay Islands, and proclaimed a protectorate over the Mosquito Indians in the period between 1823 and 1860. And their interpretation of their rights in British Guiana, and the claims they put forward to territory in this area, were to bring about a sharp controversy with the United States in 1895. In addition, they claimed an interest in Central America which led to the negotiation in 1850 of a treaty putting any future interoceanic canal under the bipartite control. None of these things, in our present perspective, seem to have done any essential damage to the United States. The claim to a protectorate over the Mosquito Indians was abandoned; the territorial claims on the British Guiana frontier were settled by arbitration; and in one of the wisest and most generous gestures of British statesmanship the exclusive right of the United States to the control of a canal was freely recognized in 1900. We need feel no resentment whatsoever over the past, but the record makes faintly absurd the view that Britain was virtuous when the nations of Continental Europe were steeped in wickedness and ambition.

So much for an examination of European intentions with regard to Latin America down to the period of the First World War. The danger to the security interests of the United States was not great, save possibly in the case of Mexico. But we need to examine this matter of security from another point of view and ask the question, regardless of what afterknowledge teaches us, as to whether the United States *thought* security interests to be involved in the evolution of the Monroe Doctrine.

There are two very striking facts with which we may begin an examination of this problem. The first is that almost never did the American government officially invoke the Doctrine in that great part of the Latin-American continents which has no contact with the Caribbean. There is, indeed, only one exception to this generalization, and this of little importance. In 1863 Spain was involved in a war with Peru, in the course of which a Spanish squadron seized the Chincha Islands. This act led Seward to instruct the American minister to Madrid to say that " the United States cannot . . . regard with indifference an attempt to reduce Peru by conquest and to re-annex its territory to the kingdom of Spain." But the warning was unnecessary. There is no evidence whatsoever that the Spanish government intended any re-establishment of its rule, and indeed the ministry disavowed such intentions almost as soon as the news of the seizure of the Chinchas reached Madrid.

Let us, then, put the generalization just made in reverse form. Speaking in practical terms, the Monroe Doctrine was for the most part a Caribbean doctrine, applying to a relatively restricted part of the Latin-American world. Here it was frequently invoked, and here, it may fairly be contended, security interests of the United States were, in the long run, involved.

In dealing with this aspect of the problem, however, there is one preliminary observation that needs to be made. In the many discussions of the Monroe Doctrine in the second half of the nineteenth century, and in the first decades of the twentieth, it is remarkable to find how little emphasis was placed, speaking generally, on the issues of national safety. No doubt the foreign offices of all countries indulge in high-sounding generalities in developing and implementing their own policies. But this fact is conspicuously true in the history of American diplomacy. Again and again, in the controversies that arose, the emphasis is on ideology, rather than on security. American statesmen have believed, and acted on the belief, that the best way to rally American opinion behind their purposes is to assert a moral principle. In doing so, they have often gone far beyond the boundaries of expediency. And perhaps it is fair to say that in underemphasizing security, they have helped to form a national habit which unduly subordinates the necessities of national defense to the assertion of lofty moral principles.

In analyzing the Caribbean doctrine, however, there is a distinction to be made. When the *canal* question is specifically under discussion, the emphasis on the physical interests of the United States becomes evident. When collateral questions are involved, the emphasis changes. Let us look at these generalizations in some detail.

The Clayton-Bulwer Treaty of 1850 was based on the assumption that an interoceanic canal would be under the auspices of both the United States and Great Britain. But, with the new consciousness of power that came with the Civil War, the American government began more and more to speak and to act as if it had an interest in the exclusive control of such a waterway. The first great debate on the problem came with

Colombia's grant to Ferdinand de Lesseps of the concession to build a canal across the Isthmus of Panama. This grant caused a very considerable to-do in the United States. In Congress, as early as June 25, 1879, Senator Ambrose Burnside of Rhode Island (the unhappy Union commander at Fredericksburg) introduced a resolution which declared that the United States "could not view without serious disquietude any attempt of the powers of Europe to establish under their protection and domination a ship canal across the Isthmus of Darien, and such action on the part of any other power could not be regarded in any other light than as the manifestation of an unfriendly disposition towards the United States." Burnside followed up this resolution with a speech in which he declared that the construction of such a canal would be dangerous to our peace and safety. This point of view was echoed by numerous persons, by such conservatives as Edwin Lawrence Godkin, the editor of *The Nation*, and Thomas Bayard, later to become Cleveland's Secretary of State. And it was strongly reiterated by President Hayes himself in his annual message of 1879. "An inter-oceanic canal," declared the President, "will essentially change the geographical relations between the Atlantic and Pacific shores of the United States and between the United States and the rest of the world.

It would be the great ocean thoroughfare between our Atlantic and Pacific shores, and virtually a part of the coastline of the United States. Our merely commercial interest in it is greater than that of all other countries, while its relation to our power and prosperity as a nation, to our means of defence, our unity, peace and safety, are matters of paramount concern to the people of the United States." It would have been difficult to have been more specific.

The language of Hayes was echoed during the administrations of Garfield and Arthur. Both Secretary James G. Blaine and Secretary Frederick T. Freylinghuysen took the same point of view. And in 1889 the Senate passed a resolution in which it was stated that " any connection of any European government with the contruction or control of any ship-canal across the Isthmus of Darien or across Central America " would be regarded " with serious disapproval " and as " injurious to the just rights and interests of the United States, and as a menace to their welfare."

It is difficult to relate the controversy over the Venezuela-British Guiana boundary in 1895 to the question of national security. For the American administration to claim an interest in that boundary has always seemed to me a very remarkable extension of the Monroe Doctrine, and one not at all necessitated by any true conception of the national interest. The possession of hundreds of square miles of uninhabited wilderness in the heart of Latin America was hardly, in my view, a matter of deep concern of the United States. But it is interesting to observe that, though the administration made nothing of the point, some of the discussion on the question turned on the possession of the mouth of the Orinoco, not unrelated to the control of the Caribbean. This was the point of view of Senator Henry Cabot Lodge; it was the point of view of Senator Zachariah Chandler. It mattered little that Great Britain had frequently offered to concede the point; in the heat of the dispute there *did* take place an attempt to relate the controversy to the security interests of the United States.

But the canal question came to the forefront of the stage again at the close of the century. And here, as is generally known, a true question of security was raised. The first Hay-Pauncefote Treaty of 1900 provided for an interoceanic canal which, though constructed by the United States, should be open to all nations, and which, so far as the text of the treaty went, should not be fortified and should be open to the vessels of all nations. But the treaty met with the most strenuous opposition, in which one of the most conspicuous figures was the then Governor of New York—Theodore Roosevelt.

To this rising politician the total control of the Canal seemed vital from the standpoint of our sea power, no less than from the standpoint of the Monroe Doctrine. The opposition of Roosevelt and others compelled John Hay to negotiate a second treaty in which the right of the United States to control the canal and to fortify it was implicitly conceded.

In the years between the second Hay-Pauncefote Treaty and the outbreak of World War I it seems certain that the canal question was in part responsible for the increasing sensitiveness of the United States with regard to the Caribbean. This sensitiveness was demonstrated when the British and the Germans blockaded the coast of Venezuela in 1902; and strategic considerations have something to do with the Roosevelt corollary to the Monroe Doctrine, with the assertion of an American right to intervene to prevent intervention by others. Were the United States to control the new interoceanic waterway, it was logical, also, that it should control the approaches to the same; and although some historians, obsessed with the economic motive, have traced the extension of the Doctrine to the bankers, a more accurate interpretation of the sudden interest of the United States in the exercise of a police power in the Caribbean lies in the strategic interests that were involved. The extension of American authority in the republics of Haiti, Santo Domingo, and Nicaragua, was essentially a cautionary policy, and it developed in a period when the possibility of a transfer of sea power from Great Britain to Germany entered into the calculations of the United States.

Per contra, it is significant that with the defeat of Germany, the Caribbean policy of the United States underwent a substantial revision. The sea power of the Reich had been destroyed; there was no European state that could or would challenge the position of the United States in the waters controlling the approaches to the Canal, and this fact explains why the Monroe Doctrine underwent substantial revision in the late twenties and the early thirties. The Roosevelt corollary was gradually abandoned. The so-called Clark memorandum on the Doctrine, written in 1928, and communicated to the Latin-American governments in 1930, explicitly repudiated the Roosevelt principle; the Senate of the United States, in approving the Kellogg-Briand pact in 1929, in a gloss which accompanied its instrument of ratification, took similar action; and still more important, in 1933 at the conference of Montevideo, the United States, under the leadership of Cordell Hull, put its name to a protocol which declared intervention by one nation in the internal affairs of another to be ipso facto illegal. This protocol, it is interesting to observe, was ratified unanimously by the Senate of the United States. In 1937, to cap the climax, an experienced Senator could describe the Doctrine as " practically obsolete."

The emergence and growth of Hitlerism produced another shift in the American attitude towards the security of the New World. It may be in this case, as in the years just before 1914, that when all the documentary evidence has been assembled (if such a thing is possible) it will be found that the German dictator was far from intending any kind of direct physical assault on Latin America. It seems clearer now than it did at the time that his vision was limited, and that his preoccupation with Europe was real and deep. But it is an entirely different thing to say, as some of our historians have been saying, that this demoniacal genius offered no possible threat to the New World. In many respects we can see things not less but more clearly today than he did then. The outstanding fact on which every thoughtful student of the period should prayerfully reflect is that the victory of Hitler, had it come about, would have been a victory leading to the development of new and terrible weapons of war that might have overawed the whole world. We do not reflect enough on the narrow margin by which this was avoided. It is true that German scientists were diverted from that type of research which finally resulted in the atomic bomb. But it is also true that the Germans did develop the rocket. Had it not been for the overrunning of their launching sites in the winter of 1945, they might have used the new weapon, V-2, with terrible effect. Had it not been for the stimulus given to our own research by the German menace and to the wise and farseeing action of a great President of the United States, they might have been in a position to dominate a large part of the world. And what a psychopathic genius, such as the Führer, would have done with the massive weapon of destruction if it had been possible for him to use it is not pleasant to contemplate. Those who belittle the wisdom of our foreign policy in the period of World War II have never, in my judgment, given sufficient notice to this fact.

It is highly intelligible, therefore, that the Roosevelt administration, in its view of the international situation as a whole, attempted to tie the states of Latin America closer to the United States. The first step (and it is worth noting that it came when many people were still complacent about the Hitlerian menace), came with President Roosevelt's visit to Buenos Aires in 1936. At the conference which he attended there, an agreement was signed calling for consultation in the event that the peace of the American Republics was menaced, and

" in the event of an international war outside America."
In addition, it was stated that " every act susceptible of
disturbing the peace of the Americas affects each and
every one of them, and justifies . . . procedure for
consultation."

This declaration, however, was only a beginning.
For no machinery was set up to give effect to these high-
sounding principles. The gap was filled at the Congress
of Lima in 1938. By this time the danger of National
Socialism was more generally recognized. Accordingly,
the nations of the New World not only reaffirmed their
solidarity " in case the peace, security or territorial
integrity of any American state " were threatened, but
they also agreed that, at the initiative of the Minister
of Foreign Affairs of any one of them, their governments would meet to consider the possibility of common
action.

The events of 1940 carried still further the movement
for common action. It is not easy to exaggerate the
impact in the United States of the events of the spring
of 1940. During the winter many Americans flattered
themselves that the war that had begun in Europe in the
fall of 1939 was a small affair, that the Allies would
win an easy victory, or that (this in the quarters most
ignorant of international matters) there was a " phony "
character to the whole business. But the months of

April, May, and June destroyed these illusions. Within
a few months the Germans invaded Norway and Den-
mark, swept relentlessly through the Netherlands and
Belgium, and brought France to her knees. What
would happen next? Could Germany, enthroned in the
Hague, claim for herself the Dutch West Indies? Could
Germany, installed in France, demand the cession of
the French Islands of the Caribbean or of French
Guiana? Would the German submarines find bases in
the New World with which to prey upon the commerce
of the democracies? It was a mark of the agitation of
the time that both houses of Congress, by a vote almost
unprecedented, passed resolutions declaring that any
transfer of territory in the New World from one
European power to another would be regarded as dangerous to the peace of the United States. Under the
impact of these events, moreover, the administration
acted with vigor. The Conference of Havana, in the
summer of 1940, was of high significance. In a remarkable declaration, the states of the New World went on
record as declaring that an attack on any one of them
must be regarded as an attack on all. A second declaration stated that " the American Republics would consider any transfer or attempt to transfer sovereignty,
jurisdiction, possession or any interest or controls in any
of these regions to another non-American state as con-

trary to American sentiments, principles and rights of American states to maintain their security and political independence," The conference went further. It provided for a scheme of international administration in case it became necessary to occupy some of the territories which might be threatened by Germany. And it declared that in an extreme emergency any American state was authorized to "take action in a manner required for its defense or the defense of the continent." Here, indeed, was a striking example of the solidarity of the states of the New World.

It was to be more than sixteen months after the declarations of the Havana Conference that the United States found itself involved in war with Germany and with Japan. In the interval the American government pressed for agreements with many of the Latin-American republics looking to the use of bases in their territory in the event of war. In some instances the bargaining was difficult. In many of the states concerned there was a latent anti-Americanism that had to be taken into consideration. A jealous regard for national sovereignty also entered into the account. But very substantial progress was made before the Japanese dropped their bombs at Pearl Harbor. For example, as early as April, 1941, the United States and Mexico entered into an agreement by which military aircraft were permitted to land in Mexican airports, and in November, Mexican ports were opened to American naval vessels. Brazil entered into a similar agreement as regards naval craft in the same month. Peru, Ecuador, and Chile all acceded to similar American requests by the autumn of 1941. Even the Panamanian government, which down to October, 1941, was in the hands of an anti-American President, joined the procession in May of 1942.

In addition to all this, once the war had come, the United States received many assurances of support from the republics of the Western hemisphere. All of them either severed relations with the Axis powers, or actually declared war. Only two of them—Chile and Argentina—were tardy in taking one or the other of these steps. Only one of them—Argentina—held out until the conflict had been decided, and by its prolonged neutrality furnished a base for Nazi espionage and intrigue. And in several instances some of the republics went further. Ecuador, for example, permitted the United States to occupy the Galapagos Islands, thus affording a new base for the protection of the Panama Canal. Brazil not only permitted the establishment of an air ferry service between its Eastern bulge and Africa, which performed an essential role in the North African campaign of 1942–43, but also sent an expeditionary force to the Italian front. Mexico dispatched an air force to the

Philippines. Taking the picture as a whole, the solidarity of the West was remarkable. It stands in striking
contrast with the situation in World War I, when such
important states as Mexico and Chile, Venezuela and
Argentina, remained neutral throughout the struggle.

Nor must we underrate the importance of Latin
America in furnishing to the United States important
strategic materials. Laurence Duggan, in his work on
The Americas, gives an interesting list of these materials.
It appears from this list that the states of the New
World supplied this country with all of its quinine
(a specific of fundamental importance in the Far Eastern
war), all of its balsa wood (significant in airplane
manufacture), all of its rotennone (a powerful insec-
ticide), 83 per cent of its imported copper, 77 per
cent of its Manila fiber, 56 per cent of its tin, 76.7 per
cent of its imported vanadium, and 43.2 per cent of its
crude rubber. Each one of these materials was a significant factor in the war effort.

The cooperative effort of the New World states in
the great struggle of 1941–45 carried over into the postwar world. The security considerations which prevailed
during the contest affected the policies of the United
States in the years that followed. Indeed, the ground-
work for a new security pattern was laid in the conference which took place in the City of Mexico in the

winter of 1945. There, the protocol of Buenos Aires, to which we have already alluded, was strengthened by a new compact, the so-called Act of Chapultepec. By this compact it was declared that an act of aggression against any one state was considered to be an act of aggression against all, and there were then enumerated the measures by which the aggressed nation would be supported. These measures were the recall of ambassadors, the severance of economic relations, the use of armed forces.

The Act of Chapultepec was adopted under war conditions, and in the view of the American delegation could be considered as binding only during the war period. To cover the ground more thoroughly, it was necessary to adopt a formal treaty, and this was done in 1947 by the Rio inter-American treaty of reciprocal assistance. By this agreement, ratified without dissent by the Senate of the United States, the contracting parties agreed, not only to take common action against aggression, but to be bound by a vote of two-thirds of the membership, except in so far as concerned the use of armed force. The principle of collective security was, in this agreement, carried further than it had been in any instance up to this time. And in requiring the United States to be bound by the vote of other nations, the Act of Rio goes even further than the North Atlantic pact of 1949.

With the Rio pact, however, we come to the culmination of the policy of collaboration in the development of American security. The question that remains for consideration is whether the course of the last ten years has not drastically altered the aspect of the security problem, and inevitably reduced the significance of the states of Latin America from the standpoint of the national defense. The question of the possible subversion of Latin-American governments is one that I shall wish to discuss in my next essay. I am speaking, it will be understood, with the physical invasion of the New World in mind. Have we not, since the year 1959, returned to very much the situation that existed in the early years of our relations with Latin America, when armed action against an American state is entirely unlikely? Is there indeed, any other area in which the prospects of such action are more remote?

In dealing with the problems of Latin-American relations, we must take account of the revolutionary changes in the international situation that have taken place since the end of the war. If the United States were again to be involved in an armed struggle, what kind of struggle would it be? Grisly as the prospect is, it *might* be all out nuclear war. But in such a war the position of our "southern neighbors" would be entirely irrelevant. The blows would likely come from bases far removed from that part of the world (the current hostile attitude of Cuba towards the United States notwithstanding), perhaps over the Pole, or from submarines discharging their lethal weapons many miles out at sea. If the struggle were more limited, what then? Obviously, the area in which we have the largest stake today is Europe. Here exists the greatest technological complex in the world, outside the United States and possibly the Soviet Union. Here lies a possible danger of conflict against which we must take every precaution. But unless operations are to be total, they must be limited. And limited operations, as a kind of symbol arising out of a threat to Europe, as an intimation of what might happen if a way were not found out of the impasse, would hardly engage the rest of the New World in direct hostilities. There are, of course, other centers of friction besides Europe. As the dispatch of troops to Lebanon in 1957 suggests, a touchy situation may arise in the Middle East. The bombardments of Quemoy and Matsu, the irreconcilable and violent nationalism of the Chinese Communists, suggest that the peace may be broken in the Far East. But in these cases, too, it is difficult to envision the role of the Latin Americans. Of course you will not misunderstand me. I am by no means saying that their good will cannot be useful to us. I am merely saying that, so far as our vision extends at the present time, there seems little reason to believe that we shall be directly threatened from the great area to the south.

There are some special aspects of the problem that deserve especial mention. One of them is the matter of our interoceanic communications. We have seen how the question of these communications gave especial vitality to the ideas of the Monroe Doctrine, and how the maximum vitality of the principles of Monroe was attained at a time when the defense of the Canal seemed to present a possible problem of high significance. In the days before 1914, the possibility of German power in the Caribbean, though much exaggerated, offered a valid argument for special vigilance. In the days of World War II, the Canal played an important part in giving mobility to our naval operations. But since then much has happened. I call your attention to a significant article appearing in *Foreign Affairs* for April, 1959. " The military value [of the Canal]," say its authors, " has been reduced both by technological developments and by new strategic developments. Although it still facilitates the efficient disposition of the Navy, there now exists a two-ocean fleet, with aircraft carriers whose beam and canted decks are too great for the Gaillard narrows. Without lessening the convenience and economy of the Canal's facilities for bulk cargo, the growth of continental means of transportation on land and in the air, has provided a more adequate alternative to meet the needs of swift wartime mobilization. High speed highways and jet-propelled military and civilian aircraft transports link the east and west coast with rapid services. Continental pipelines transporting oil at a cost comparable to that of tankers have cut into the value of inter-coastal trade carried by the Canal. Moreover, the industrial development of the west coast has diverted petroleum products to local consumption. Despite apparent obstacles, it is not impossible that the Arctic Ocean may in time provide an alternative strategic route which will cut nearly 5000 miles from the 11,200 miles separating the ports of Tokyo and London."

Nor is this by any means the whole of the story. The protection of the Canal is an entirely different matter than it was in the course of World War II. One may wonder indeed whether any measures could be taken that would guarantee its safety. There are eminent military analysts who believe that it could not be defended at all in total war, and that it would be more difficult to defend than ever before in a limited war. The forces protecting the Canal Zone today are merely skeletal. The military people themselves appear to have written down its importance.

Turn the matter about, and we come to the same conclusion. Since the Canal is no longer of major importance in the waging of war, it is not at all likely to be one of the first enemy targets. There are other ways of inflicting damage on this country far more important than the interruption of its interoceanic traffic. If we come to a large-scale struggle in the future, it is likely that a few swift strokes at the great cities of the country will be the objectives of the enemy.

Messrs. Travis and Watkins, in their article in *Foreign Affairs*, deduce from the facts just mentioned that it would be wise to put the Canal under the control of a special commission, under the aegis of the United Nations. American public opinion is, by no means, prepared for such a step today; the recent injudicious conduct of the Panamanian hotheads has done nothing to make such a step easier; the conclusions of Travis and Watkins are more difficult to accept than their hypothesis. But it is important for us to understand that the defense policies of two decades ago may be totally irrelevant in the climate of the sixties.

There is another aspect of the question of national security that demands consideration and in which outmoded thinking again played a part. In the last years of the war the American military chiefs attached great importance to the standardization of the armed forces of the American republics. In October of 1945 the Inter-American Defense Board recommended to the governments that they " adopt as their ultimate objective the full standardization of the materiel of all units of the various armed forces and the facilities for its production," that they assure " adequate capacitation of human resources through measures such as compulsory military service, preliminary training, formation of cadres and so forth," that they adopt uniform training methods, and that exchanges of officers and students be instituted.

In 1946 President Truman suggested to Congress the implementation of these recommendations and the passage of an Inter-American Military Cooperation Act. This act would have made possible not only the exchange of students mentioned, but also the exchange of modern American equipment for the armaments at that time posessed by the states of Latin America. Just precisely what useful purpose would be served by rearming the Latin Americans at the end of a world struggle it was difficult for some of us to perceive. The proposal met with a mixed reception from the Latin American Republics. It was most favorably viewed by those states where the military were in control; it was

viewed with suspicion in some other quarters, notwithstanding President Truman's declaration that it would
be necessary to " guard against placing weapons in the
hands of any groups which may use them to oppose
the peaceful and democratic principles to which the
United States and other American nations have so often
subscribed." Fortunately, as I view the matter, the
American Congress took a dim view of the Military
Cooperation Act, and it was never enacted into law.

The history of military assistance to Latin-American
states confirms the wisdom of this decision. In the past,
sales, sometimes innocently entered into, of military
equipment to one of these states has been followed by
heart-burnings in another. The possibilities of a sense-
less and even dangerous arms competition would only
be enhanced by legislation of the type that the President
suggested. There was also the collateral danger that
the influence of the armed forces would be enhanced.
There are states in Latin America where, for the time
being, the army may be a necessary and stabilizing
element. But in general, it is not in the interest of the
United States to increase the influence of the military
in this part of the world, or to stimulate rivalries that
are latent in the relations of these republics. Moreover,
to dole out armaments might easily make the United
States a detested umpire in an American armaments

race, produce the spectacle of other American citizens being killed with arms coming from the United States, and place an undue burden upon the economies of the countries concerned. It is the policy of the United States to reduce armaments by international agreement rather than to encourage their growth.

More limited agreements with Latin-American states may be another matter. While, as I have said, the character of the next war, if it comes, may very well be quite different from that of the last, the grant of arms for specific purposes related to the defense of the hemisphere, such as arms for the protection of the coast, for marine antisubmarine or air patrol, seem innocent enough. Such grants have now been made to a substantial number of the republics. An even more positive view may be taken of training missions, either of the dispatch of American officers to other American states, or of Latin-American officers to the United States. It is true that the late Laurence Duggan, in his interesting book, *The Americas*, took a dim view of any such contact. Speaking of the Latin-American military caste, he wrote in 1949: " This caste does not and cannot believe in democracy, whatever lip service it pays, because true democracy would mean transformation of the society which selects and supports it. This caste admires United States technology but scorns the anti-

militaristic attitude of our people and subjection of our
army to the demands of public opinion."

Duggan's point of view deserves respect, but it does
not necessarily require acceptance. Not all Latin-
American military men are of the type described.
Furthermore, it is perhaps not too optimistic to assume
that contact with the American military would tend
to increase their understanding of the democratic view.
Nothing is more striking than the attitude of the great
majority of our own army and navy officers. They are
not only far divorced from any desire to dominate
politics; they are not only deeply devoted to democratic
principles; they are again and again the friends of
decent international relationships. It is entirely possible,
though of course not probable, that increasing contacts
between our own soldiers and those of Latin America
would have favorable and not unfavorable consequences. There are signs that in Latin America there
is a growing disposition on at least a part of the
military caste to recognize their responsibilities to favor
the democratic processes. There have been numerous
instances in recent years where the armed forces have
sustained and strengthened the forces of democracy.
Contact with our own soldiers and sailors is, in my
judgment, likely to do them more good than harm.

May I, in closing, again revert to the philosophical

implications of what I have had to say? The determination of the security interests of a great nation is not a mathematical matter, nor is it a constant in international affairs. It is possible grossly to exaggerate the danger to this country, as Monroe did in 1823. He was saved from the possible consequences of his famous declaration by the fact that there was not the slightest danger of the conquest of the newborn nations from any European power. He was propounding a point of view that, in terms of logistics, had very little to be said for it.

Practically speaking, moreover, the United States for long generations did nothing to implement Monroe's declaration. It was content with a meager army and a meager navy. The high-sounding phrases in which the President proclaimed the defense of the New World had no effect in the actual development of the defense policies of the United States. They illustrate the gulf between the pious declaration and the preparation for action that has from time to time, and not happily, characterized the diplomacy of this nation. The lesson is a far-reaching one. We need nothing more in this country than a clear realtionship of means to end. This a great deal of writing about the Monroe Doctrine has not supplied.

There was, however, as we have seen, a genuine

relationship between the Doctrine, as applied to the Caribbean, and the strategic interests of the country. The Doctrine was most closely geared to reality in the years at the turn of the century and of World War I. It lost significance in the twenties and early thirties, but regained importance with the rise of Hitlerism.

Today, however, a totally different situation has arisen. It is not likely that the conventional view of the defense problem will be easily put aside. Men are sometimes instructed by the past, and sometimes its prisoners. The latter may well be true of much thinking of our own time. In reality, the defense of the West rests on different assumptions than that which envisages direct attack. The real enemy in the Western hemisphere is not invasion, but the penetration of the alien and vicious ideas that emanate from the Kremlin. The real questions to be asked are two. Can Latin America become in spirit and in fact the citadel of democracy, as in all good faith Monroe and Henry Clay dreamed that it would be 120 odd years ago? Can it, in the development of its economic life, recognize the values of the free society, strengthen its ties with the United States, and go forward along lines that emphasize its community of interest and thought with the nations of the West? To carry the questioning further: Can it resist in the political and economic sphere the blandishments and seductions of Moscow? Is it on these grounds that the battle of the future will be fought, not on the basis of invasion or of conquest? I shall give a partial answer to these questions in the following essays.

LATIN-AMERICAN POLITICAL
RELATIONS WITH THE
UNITED STATES

THE HISTORY OF our political relationship with the Latin-American states may be divided into several periods. First comes the period of the colonial revolts. Second, extending from about 1826 to the end of the Civil War, comes a period of relative estrangement. Third comes a period of renewed interest in the last two decades of the century. Fourth comes a period beginning in the first of the 1900's in which the United States attempted to intervene directly in the affairs of many of the republics of the New World. Then comes the period of the good neighbor. And last comes the contemporary period, which we shall not attempt to characterize in a phrase, but in which many crosscurrents are visible.

In considering the first of these periods, the period of colonial revolt, we must first of all remind ourselves that in the 1820's the United States was, in the eyes of many Europeans, as radical a threat to the existing order as is the regime of the Kremlin today. The prevailing doctrine on the continent of Europe was the doctrine of legitimacy. It was the doctrine that the authority of the sovereign rested on a firm foundation of moral right, and could not legitimately be overthrown. The thesis was never better stated than by the great Metternich, in commenting to the Tsar Alexander on the Monroe Doctrine. "These United States of America," he wrote, "which we have seen arise and grow, and which during their too short youth already mediated projects which they dared not then avow, have suddenly left a sphere too narrow for their ambition, and have astonished Europe by a new act of revolt, more unprovoked, fully as audacious, and no less dangerous than the former. They have distinctly and clearly announced their intention to set, not only power against power, but, to put it more exactly, altar against altar. In their indecent declarations they have cast blame and scorn on the institutions of Europe most worthy of respect, on the principles of their greatest sovereigns, on the whole of those measures which a sacred duty no less than an evident necessity has forced our governments to adopt to frustrate plans most criminal. In permitting themselves these unprovoked attacks, in fostering revolutions wherever they show themselves, in regretting those which have failed, in extending a helping hand to those which seem to prosper, they lend new strength to the apostles of sedition, and re-animate the courage of every conspirator. If this flood of pernicious example should extend over the whole of America, what would become of our religious and political institutions, of the moral force of our governments, and of the conservative system which has saved Europe from complete dissolution?"

By contrast with this view, the United States actually welcomed the downfall of colonialism in the New World. Mindful of their own past and of their relatively recent overthrow of British rule, many Americans watched with sympathy the course of events in the lands of the South. The demand for recognition of the new republics arose as early as 1818, and was eloquently voiced by Henry Clay. If the Monroe administration proceeded with greater caution, it was because it was engaged in negotiations with Spain for the cession of the Floridas, negotiations which were finally brought to an end only in 1821. Even so, it was the first government outside the Latin-American area to recognize the new states, and its action was, in a very real sense, a defiance to the nations of Continental Europe. The audacity of the move has been little appreciated.

In coming to their decision, Monroe and his advisers were most certainly guided and influenced by ideological considerations. Such considerations have again

and again played an important part in the formation
of American foreign policy. We fail to understand the
character of that policy if we do not take full account
of the strength of moral convictions and sentimental
predilections in the evolution of our diplomacy. The
ideological motive is strongly stressed in the language
of Monroe's famous message of 1823. " The political
system of the Allied powers," wrote Monroe, " is essentially different . . . from that of America. This dif-
ference proceeds from that which exists in their respec-
tive governments." And again, " It is impossible that
the allied powers should extend their political system
to any portion of either continent without endangering
our peace and safety; nor can anyone believe that our
southern brethren, if left to themselves, would adopt
it of their own accord." It is to be found also in the
speeches of Henry Clay. " I am inclined to believe,"
said Clay as early as 1818, " that they will establish
free governments. We are their great example. Of us
they constantly speak as brothers. They adopt our
principles, copy our institutions, and in many instances,
employ the very language and sentiments of our revolutionary papers. But it is sometimes said that they are
too ignorant and superstitious to admit of the existence
of free government. . . . It is the doctrine of thrones

that man is too ignorant to govern himself. Self-government is the natural government of man."

But along with the ideological motive, there was another motive for the recognition of the former Spanish colonies and for the enunciation of the Monroe Doctrine. It does not appear in Monroe's message; it is not stressed in any of his correspondence. But it clealy appears in the thought and in the language of John Quincy Adams. As a New Englander, Adams was naturally interested in the foreign commerce of the United States. He had protested against the ukase of the Tsar which barred American commerce from a large part of the Northwest Coast. He had taken steps in his first instructions to the ministers sent out to Latin America to stress the importance of opening the door to American enterprise. He had inveighed against the principle of colonialism as " an abuse of government." He was clearly aware of the economic interest involved in the independence of the colonies. As so often in the history of American diplomacy, self-interest and idealism combined to give coherence and strength to the enunciation of policy.

The pronouncement of 1823, however, was not followed by a close association of the United States with the new republics. Indeed, the period from 1826 to the end of the Civil War was, broadly considered, a period in which American interest in Latin America was far from keen, and in which enthusiasm for the United States in Latin America was far from widespread.

The development of Latin America in the first forty years of independence could hardly be said to have justified the optimistic prediction of Henry Clay. Adams, hard-boiled and realistic, had from the beginning mistrusted those predictions. Speaking in 1821, he said: " I have seen and yet see no prospect that they will establish free or liberal institutions of government. . . . They have not the first element of good government. Arbitrary power, military and ecclesiastical, is stamped upon their education, upon their habits and upon all their institutions. Nor is there any appearance of a disposition to take any political lessons from us." This view, unhappily enough, was largely justified by subsequent events. Without any tradition of self-rule, with ignorant and illiterate populations, with wide social cleavages between the governing class and the mass of the people, with the ascendancy of the military classes which had been responsible for the success of the revolutions, many, indeed most, of the Latin American states sank into disorder, or came under the sway of military despots. These general conditions naturally reduced enthusiasm in the United States for the new republics, and they were accompanied, oftentimes, by diplomatic controversies which did not improve the atmosphere.

In reflecting on these developments, it is worthwhile to relate them to the present. There are optimists today who look upon the end of colonialism in Africa as ushering in an era of peace and democracy. But is it not more likely that the experience of the Dark Continent will be that of Latin America? With racial and tribal divisions and rivalries, with a shallow economic base, with widespread illiteracy, is it reasonable to believe that the next fifty years will see genuine political freedom or perfect tranquillity? I think not.

This, of course, is a parenthesis. Let us return to the matter of American relations with the republics of the South. The Monroe Doctrine was hardly more than a flash in the pan. For two decades after its enunciation, the United States pursued a course of disassociation from Latin America. Monroe's message had suggested close ties of friendship. But the brave language of the President was soon repudiated. When in 1824 and 1825, four nations, one after the other, appealed to the government of the United States for an alliance, they were answered in the negative. The administration would not have dared commit itself so far, despite the applause with which, in general, the message had been received. Moreover, firm opposition to any entanglement with the new republics expressed itself in Congress in 1826. President Adams recommended on this occasion the dispatch of American representatives to a Congress of Latin American nations to be held at Panama. The opposition at the Capitol was very lively. And one thing stood out above all others in the debates —opposition to any political commitments to the new states.

The policies of the administrations which followed Monroe and Adams were concerned with other issues than those which related to Latin America. In the thirties and the early forties little is heard of the Monroe Doctrine. In 1845, in his message to the Congress, President James Polk declared that the Doctrine applied with " greatly increased force " to the North American continent, a backhanded way of reducing responsibility for its enforcement in other areas. And though in the Central-American area the Doctrine figured in the fifties, it was still a matter of partisan debate until at least 1855. In the Pan-American conferences of this period, if the word Pan-American be not too large a word to describe these partial and ineffective gatherings, the United States was not represented. It sent no one to the Congress of Lima in 1846; the Congress at Santiago in 1856 was hardly noticed by it; and William H. Seward was not willing to have the American government take a part in the conference at Lima in 1865.

The political indifference of the United States to our " southern brethren " was matched by the lack of enthusiasm in Latin America for the United States. After all, it was widely recognized in the southern continent that the power which stood in the path of the Holy Alliance (always assuming that some nefarious enterprise was in the wind) was Great Britain, not the republic in the West. And as time went on, the conduct of the United States could hardly arouse warm sentiments of regard in the republics of the continent. The war with Mexico was widely regarded as a war of aggression, and no doubt was all the more so because of the opposition to the conflict in the American Congress. In the fifties there came the era of the filibusters. In the middle fifties, William Walker, a soldier of fortune, not only invaded Nicaragua, but actually set up a government there, and became President himself. He was before long overthrown, but his enterprise could hardly be expected to produce sentiments of friendship in the breasts of the Latin Americans.

There is, perhaps, one other element in the problem that ought to be mentioned. The contacts of the intelligentsia of the new republics were, in this period, much more frequently with Europe than with the United

States. The record of Latin-American travel to this country during the period is extremely meager. While closer cultural contacts do not inevitably produce closer political relations, the absence of such contacts, a kind of intellectual isolationism, is certainly not the soil in which an effective rapprochement can grow.

With the American Civil War, however, a change in the political climate begins, ushering in a new period of closer association and greater cordiality. The war itself had something to do with this fact. The vitality of democratic institutions seemed confirmed by the victory of the North. The abolition of slavery was a great act that could not fail to make its impression on the Latin Americans, all the more so since slavery had been abolished in many cases in their own states. The determined stand taken by the United States against the French intervention in Mexico no doubt added to American prestige. Finally, the years after the war were the years of the heyday of republicanism as a gospel. Today, sophisticated people fully realize that democracy and monarchy are not incompatible, and that the most democratic people in Europe operate under monarchical forms. This was by no means so clear eighty or ninety years ago. At that time republicanism still had about it a certain aura, and the United

States, as the greatest of all republics, a certain attractive power.

The growth of more cordial relations between the United States and our southern brethren deserves fuller analysis than it has as yet received at the hands of scholars. Professor Arthur P. Whitaker in his admirable book *The Western Hemisphere Idea,* published only a few years ago, has thrown much light on the subject, however. We may begin by saying that a new enthusiasm for America is discernible in Latin America before the complementary movement sets in here at home. Take, for example, the case of Argentina. Here, the great name in connection with the new attitude is the name of Domingo Sarmiento, who, after an active career in Argentine politics and a visit to this country in 1847, was Minister to the United States from 1865–68, and President of the Argentine Republic from 1868 to 1874. Much disillusioned by his travels in Europe, which seemed to him to provide no program for the improvement of society, and deeply discontented with the political developments in Latin America, Sarmiento came to the conclusion that the regenerative elements in contemporary politics were to be found in the American republic. At the same time he found in closer relations with the great republic of the North the hope of larger economic development.

Sarmiento was not alone. Another Argentine, Juan Batista Alberdi, in a much-read book published in 1870 entitled *The Crime of War*, drew the conclusion that the day of international conflict was drawing to a close, and saw in the federation of the two Americas the first step towards the development of a world society. The Chilean José Victorino Lastarria stressed the dissociation of America from Europe, and resentfully sought to rebut the charge that the peoples of the New World were of an inferior race. Another Chilean, Francisco Bilbao, wrote in the same vein.

Before we leave this angle of the subject, we must place the whole matter of the Latin American attitude toward democracy in a clear light. It is, of course, true that very few Latin-American states can match the ordered progress of the United States in the fulfillment of the ideal popular government. But what is often overlooked is that powerful sentiment in favor of the democratic ideal has for a long time existed in Latin America, and that it has grown rather than receded. As a learned student of the matter once said to me, " If the Latin Americans are not democrats, they want to be." But I shall return to this matter later.

Contemporaneously with the development of a more sympathetic attitude toward the United States in the lands to the south, there went the development of a corresponding attitude in this country. And as in the early period, sentiment and interest combined to produce this result. On the side of sentiment, the same feeling that republicanism was somehow inherently superior to monarchy operated in favor of cordial relations. The dogma of the two spheres that lay behind the Monroe Doctrine, and that had become stronger than ever in the years succeeding the Civil War, operated in the same direction.

The belief that the New World should be insulated from the follies and wickednesses of the Old was widespread throughout the nineteenth century and had a part in the development of the Pan-American idea. But at the same time more practical motives entered into the account. It was to be some time before the foreign trade of the United States bulked large in the calculations of statesmen. Yet that trade was increasing in the seventies and eighties, and the South-American market seemed to offer great opportunities to American enterprise. The enterprise of De Lesseps, with its possible suggestion of European influence in the New World, made more expedient a closer relationship. The existence of two large-scale wars in South America, the conflict between Paraguay and Brazil, Argentina and Uruguay, and between Chile, Bolivia and Peru, pointed up the desirability of American machinery for the maintenance of peace. It was considerations such as these that led James G. Blaine in 1881 to propose a conference of the American nations to meet in Washington. Before anything could come of this, the assassination of President Garfield removed Blaine from office, but the idea that he had fostered nonetheless gained strength in the eighties, and was propagated by men such as William McKinley, John T. Morgan of Alabama, the sturdy advocate of a Nicaraguan canal, Hinton Rowan Helper, and William Eleroy Curtis. Their active labors culminated in a congressional resolution of 1888, which called upon the President to summon an inter-American conference. This conference met in 1889.

Among the stated purposes of the conference was the development of an American customs union. So grandiose an idea was not then, and is not now, possible. It was rejected by an overwhelming vote. Yet the conference was by no means barren. It drew up an arbitration convention for the settlement of disputes between American states. It set up the Commercial Bureau of the American Republics in Washington, which was in time to develop into the Pan-American Union. This agency for many years kept out of political questions, but it brought together much useful information on the Latin-American Republics, and provided not only special studies of many aspects of Latin-American life, but another means of association between Latin Americans and North Americans.

By comparison with the preceding period, then, the eighties and the early nineties were years of developing contact. But it must not be imagined that they were years of really close association. Latin America has rarely viewed the United States without some reserve. This country is too powerful not to waken apprehension, and the tone of its diplomatic correspondence, no less than the utterances of its public men, has sometimes wounded Latin-American susceptibilities. For example, in 1895, when Grover Cleveland demanded of Great Britain that she arbitrate her boundary dispute with Venezuela over the British Guiana boundary, the re-action of the Latin-American states was not invariably enthusiastic. Richard Olney, in his famous note of July 20, with sublime disregard of the feelings of others, had proclaimed that the " fiat of the United States was law on the American continents on the subjects to which it confined its interposition," and the phrase jarred the feelings of many of our " southern neighbors." In Chile, in Mexico, in the Argentine, the general reception of the message was chilly. When the government of Ecuador, a much weaker state, suggested a Congress to give " to the American doctrine, initiated with so much glory by the illustrious Monroe, all the extension which it deserves, and the necessary guarantees to make it respected," its proposal met with a decidedly cool reception.

Olney's language, indeed, reflects the growing nationalism of the United States at the turn of the century. One effect of this nationalism was the growth of feeling that the blessings of the American way of life ought to be imposed on others, if they were not voluntarily accepted. Putting the matter in other terms, the first decades of the twentieth century are the decades of North American imperialism. In this short period, the United States, in at least five instances, asserted a right of control over five of the " sister republics " of the West.

The first instance in which this was done was Cuba. Having freed Cuba from the Spaniards, Americans began to wonder whether after all the Cubans were fit for self-government. When our forces withdrew from the island in 1902, we extorted from the new state treaty recognition of our right to intervene, " for the preservation of Cuban independence, the maintenance of a government adequate for the protection of liberty and property, and individual liberty," and for discharging our " obligation with regard to Cuba." True, so far as actual reoccupation of the island was concerned, we acted only once, and that for a brief time (1906–1909), and at the request of the Cubans themselves. But the feeling that we had a special responsibility to see that the Cubans behaved was expressed in other ways by succeeding administrations, and the agreement cited above implied a very clear limitation on Cuban sovereignty.

Soon thereafter, we asserted a right of control over another newborn state. It is not necessary here to relate in detail the circumstances which gave birth to the Republic of Panama. Suffice it to say that when the Panamanians revolted from the government of Colombia, the United States not only interposed in a way which made the repression of the revolt impossible, but also recognized the new republic with what has often been condemned as indecent haste. Recognition was followed by a treaty, and in that treaty the American government was given a qualified right to intervene in Panama and to exercise in the Canal Zone all the rights of a sovereign power.

The interventionist viewpoint was again expressed only a year after the signing of the treaty with Panama. President Roosevelt had observed with malaise the apprehension created in the United States by the Anglo-German blockade of Venezuela in 1902–1903. Reflecting upon the matter, and prodded by the British, he evolved the theory that came to be known as the

Roosevelt corollary to the Monroe Doctrine. "Chronic wrong-doing," he said in his message of 1904, "may in America, as elsewhere, ultimately require intervention by some civilized power, and in the Western Hemisphere the adherence of the United States to the Monroe Doctrine may force the United States, however reluctantly, in flagrant cases of such wrong-doing or impotence, to the exercise of an international police power." In 1905, in accordance with this theory, the Dominican government was by a show of force persuaded to hand over the control of its customs to the United States.

It was not difficult to extend the new theory. The Taft administration negotiated a similar treaty with Nicaragua, and when obstacles to its execution arose, landed the marines, who stayed in that little republic with a brief interruption until 1933. The Wilson administration, no doubt animated by the purest of motives, intervened in Haiti in 1915, and there the marines remained until 1934; and finally, the anarchical conditions existing in the Dominican Republic brought about an occupation which lasted until 1924. None of these interventions was accomplished without resistance; and in Haiti and in the Dominican Republic substantial losses were sustained in guerrilla warfare.

Since Americans from time to time fall victim to the temptation to reform the conduct of others, it may be worthwhile to examine the actual results of these various cases of tutelage and of occupation. Is this the proper recipe for the extension of democratic principles in the New World?

Before we answer this question we may say that American policy had some beneficial results. At a minimum, orderly financing followed on American control. In Cuba, in Haiti, and in the Dominican Republic, the extension of education was an important by-product of the occupations. In the same three republics, an extensive road-building program was carried on. In Cuba and in Haiti, most laudable efforts were made to deal with the problems of public health, with substantial results. But in so far as democratic government is concerned, what is the record?

Cuba, in the fifty years, since the second withdrawal of the Americans, has had its ups and downs. There have been some honest elections and some decent regimes. But there was rarely a more repulsive dictatorship in any Latin-American country than that of Gerardo Machado, and though President Fulgencio Batista practiced a policy of relative tolerance in his first presidential term, his later incumbency was marred by severe measures of repression. The conduct of Fidel Castro today, whatever we may think of his economic policies or his ideals, can hardly be described as consistent with democratic principles.

Panama has been the scene of less violence and no such unsavory figure as Machado has ever appeared in its history. Yet it has not been free from revolutionary disturbances or from strong-arm rule, such as that exercised by the late Colonel Remón. In Nicaragua, after an occupation that had lasted thirteen years, the process of orderly election was soon repudiated. After our second intervention, we succeeded in preparing the way for a presidential contest which was waged under what we would consider the rules of the game. But we had not long been out of Nicaragua before the ambitious chief of the constabulary which we had created for the maintenance of order, seized the supreme power. This was Anastasio Somoza, who remained in office until his assassination in 1955. And he has been succeeded by one of his sons, who is hardly conducting himself according to democratic rules. What of Santo Domingo? There, too, when we withdrew there was an election which measured up to democratic standards after a fashion. But within six years of our withdrawal, the head of the constabulary seized the supreme power, and he has been the dominating figure in the history of the republic ever since. No one would claim that the result had been a great gain for democracy.

The story is little more encouraging in Haiti. There the American protectorate lasted longer than in either of the other two states just mentioned. The result has certainly not been orderly democratic rule. Neither has it been the secure establishment of a dictatorship. It has been dictatorship, punctuated by revolution. And today the state of the Haitian republic is not appreciably different, so far as democracy is concerned, from what it was when we first intervened.

The regulatory spirit expressed in the intervention was illustrated in another expedient to ensure regular and free elections in the republics of Latin America. This was to withhold recognition from governments which have come into power by unconstitutional means. The first important instance of the application of this principle was in the treaties of 1907 with regard to the states of Central America. By these treaties the signatory powers, including the United States, agreed that they would not acknowledge any government which came into power as the result of a *coup d'état* until it had received the approval of the electorate in a fair and free election. But this did not prevent revolutions from taking place. Central America was in turmoil in the years 1909 to 1912, and it is not of record that the treaties of 1907 substantially affected the situation. It was easy for a revolutionary regime to manufacture elections that confirmed its power, and such regimes were readily recognized by their neighbors.

The same experiment, with regard to Central America, was tried again through new treaties in 1923. For a brief period these treaties produced relative tranquility, but in 1931 an ambitious soldier, Maximiliano Martinez by name, seized power in El Salvador. He went unrecognized for a season, but when it became clear that he had firmly established his rule, one by one the states of Central America recognized him, and the treaties of 1923 collapsed much as the treaties of 1907 had done.

There are other even more instructive examples of the danger and futility of the policy of nonrecognition. One of these is to be found in President Wilson's policy towards Mexico. When Wilson entered power in 1913, he found just established at Mexico City a government which owed its origins to a *coup d'état* by a hardened soldier, Victoriano Huerta. He announced that he would not recognize such a regime. What was the result? The President found himself led on to a policy of partiality towards Huerta's Mexican rivals. What is more, when there occurred at Tampico a trivial incident involving the temporary detention by a Huerta subordinate of a small naval party belonging to an American warship, Wilson demanded an apology. And when, as was to be expected, the Huerta regime boggled, and in addition, it was discovered that a cargo of arms to the regime was on the way to Mexico, the President ordered the occupation of Vera Cruz. The eventual result was the overthrow of the Huerta regime; but there was in the whole episode the risk of war, and of a war that would hardly have been to the advantage of the United States. Nor was the regime which the American government assisted to come to power a democratic regime in any sense of the term. Once again the policy of nonrecognition had failed.

In 1944, even though it comes at a later period than that we are considering, the Argentine government was falling more and more under the control of reactionary forces controlled by the military. In that year there came into power a regime headed by one Edelmiro Farrell. The United States declined to recognize this government. (It had, of course, an additional grievance against it besides its nondemocratic character. The new administration was oriented towards the Axis.) Was the policy successful? It was not. True, the Farrell regime was in due course succeeded by the regime of Colonel Juan Perón. And Perón won in what was generally regarded as a fair election. But one of the reasons for his triumph in all probability was the resentment awakened by the attitude of the United States. In particular, when the American ambassador at Buenos

Aires flagrantly intervened in the domestic politics of the republic, in the name of democracy, he produced a strong popular reaction. " Braden ó Perón " was the election cry. The Argentine people responded by giving a great electoral majority to a man who became one of the most unlovely figures in the history of Latin-American politics and one of the most disastrous to the people of his country. Taken all in all, it is probably right to say that nonrecognition actually strengthens a revolutionary regime in most instances, that it enables that regime to beat the big bass drum of nationalism and to represent itself to the people as gallantly defending them against the intrusions of the foreigner. One may even go further and say that it is not only ineffective in most cases, but that it arouses resentment in other Latin-American states, as well as in the state against which it is directed.

Intervention and nonrecognition are only two of the ways in which the United States, in the period 1902–33, attempted to influence the conduct of the states of the Caribbean. In the case of Cuba, for example, the American government often sought to bring moral pressure upon the Cuban government, treating it as a kind of unruly offspring; in 1920, at the request of the regime in power, it sent observers to the island to police the elections, and in 1921 it brought economic pressure to bear to institute economic and political reforms. This pressure took the form of closing the money market to the government until it had set its house in order. The expedient was not particularly successful. The Cubans made the demanded reforms, took the money, and then reverted to their previous practices.

What derives from our brief survey of the effects of American efforts to regulate the affairs of our neighbors? No careful student would deduce from that survey that the interposition of the United States in the affairs of other nations had resulted in any very sweeping change in their political habits or in the secure establishment of popular rule. Compare this story with the story of American policy toward Mexico. With regard to Mexico, the American government showed great restraint in the second and third decades of the century when it was interfering elsewhere. It is true that the Wilson administration gave the orders for the occupation of Vera Cruz. But it steadfastly resisted the pressure—and the temptation—to engage in all-out intervention, and in the twenties, despite the threat to American economic interests in Mexico, a similar policy was followed. And today? Of all the states of the Caribbean area Mexico is the most stable, the most intelligently progressive, the nearest to popular rule (with the exception of Costa Rica). Is it not clear, then, that we must trust rather to internal forces than to external pressure in hoping for the gradual strengthening of democracy in the lands to the south? Decidedly, I would say.

The policy of the " civilizing mission," as Professor Whitaker has called it, was never popular in Latin America. Signs of resentment at the policies of the United States appeared at the Pan-American Conference at Santiago in 1923. But they were much more fully and vehemently expressed at the Havana Conference in 1928. In 1927 an inter-American Commission of Jurists had adopted a formula that " no state could interfere in the domestic affairs of another." Forewarned that the question would be discussed at the Havana Conference, the administration called upon one of the greatest of Americans, Charles Evans Hughes, to come to its defense. Hughes succeeded in preventing any action directly critical of the United States. But thirteen of the twenty-one states at the conference made it clear that they supported the formula of the Commission in principle, and eight states took an even stronger position. Though a vote on the question was postponed, it was clear that the American government was very decidedly on the defensive.

But new tendencies had been developing in American

policy. The policy of intervention had never been widely popular, and in 1925 we had withdrawn from the Dominican Republic. In 1925 we had attempted withdrawal from Nicaragua, and though we went in again, after supervised elections, we again withdrew in 1933. In 1928 there was drawn up in the State Department the so-called Clark memorandum, which expressly repudiated the Roosevelt corollary to the Monroe Doctrine, and in 1930 the contents of this memorandum were communicated to the Latin-American republics. In the meantime, the Senate of the United States, in adding a gloss to the resolution of ratification of the Kellogg-Briand pact, limited the Doctrine in much the same fashion. Things were obviously moving in the direction of a new orientation. This new orientation was more fully revealed in the first years of the New Deal.

The conferences of Montevideo and Buenos Aires set the seal on the new policy. At Montevideo, Secretary Hull agreed to a protocol which, in language more sweeping than that of the Commission of Jurists, prohibited interference in the "internal or external affairs" of the signatories. He did, however, boggle a bit at the language of the protocol, and in 1936 at the Conference of Buenos Aires, the Latin Americans returned again to the charge. There a new protocol was adopted, which declared " inadmissible " the intervention of any American state in the affairs of another, " directly or indirectly, and for whatever reason." This protocol, like the preceding one, significantly enough, was ratified unanimously by the Senate of the United States.

We should pause for a moment to underline the high importance of these two documents. Our Latin-American critics have spoken, and rightly, of American imperialism. But they have rarely remembered how brief was the period in which the United States sought to exercise direct control over the affairs of any Latin-American state, and still less have they remarked upon the unusual spectacle of a great and powerful nation binding itself in unequivocal fashion by a solemn international engagement to abstain from the use of force in a wide area. The pledges given are now more than twenty years old. Certainly, in so far as physical intervention is concerned, they have been scrupulously kept. It will be agreed, I think, that this is no light thing.

The adoption of the nonintervention principle opens an era of cordial relations between the United States and the nations of Latin America. No doubt there were other reasons why the thirties and early forties were distinguished by closer understanding between the colossus of the North and the other American nations than at any other time. Pan-Americanism fitted well with the isolationist sentiment dominant in the early thirties, and with the revulsion against closer association with Europe that came in the same period, and was accentuated by the depression. On the other hand, from the Latin-American point of view, the importance of the United States was underlined by the rise of German National Socialism. As we have already seen, it did not prove difficult for American statesmanship to evoke the idea of a common interest in protecting the New World against the ambitions of Hitlerian Germany. The steps by which the American nations were drawn together as the shadows of war loomed larger we have already reviewed. There were, it is true, rifts in the lute. The growing rapprochement of the United States with the nations to the south was watched with a jaundiced eye by many elements in the Argentine republic. The distrust of American hegemony was not entirely removed. But the general picture was highly favorable.

We may turn, then, to the postwar era and see what major lines of tendency we can discern in connection with this period. What are the principal questions that deserve discussion? Along what lines is the policy of the United States to be directed? What are the dangers of the future? How shall we estimate them?

It is apparent, on the most superficial observation,

that new currents are flowing in Latin America. As in other parts of the world, there is a strong desire to develop a more vigorous and more diversified economy, to raise the standard of living, and to create a society which more nearly corresponds to some ideal conception of distributing justice. In many of the more advanced states there is a powerful labor movement. There is also a reaction against the traditional pattern of government, in so far as that pattern exalted the influence of the military and resulted in the establishment of authoritarian regimes. There is a vigorous spirit of nationalism, which insists upon the recognition of the importance of Latin America in world affairs and is sometimes expressed in hostility to the foreign entrepreneur and vigorous dislike of interference from outside. These are some of the factors that have been revealed in the decade and a half since the war.

Many of these factors involve questions of economics, and with them I shall try to deal in my closing essay. But many of them are questions of high politics.

First of all, what should be the position of the United States with regard to the internal regimes of the Latin-American states? Should it deal on a purely objective basis with them? Or should it discriminate between those which are moving in the direction of democracy and those which remain under personal rule?

There has been a division of opinion on this question during the last decade. One view is that we should consider the question solely from the view of these interests: if it preserves order and protects the American investor, and does not impose on him excessive burdens, then, so the argument runs, why not deal with it? Why not recognize the hard practical facts of the situation? Is it not likely indeed that some of these authoritarian regimes will be easier to do business with than the democratic or quasi-democratic governments which are amongst the alternatives? Are they not a useful barrier against Communism?

This view has been more than once expressed in practice. The relations of the American ambassador in Cuba with the now-ousted dictator, Fulgencio Batista, appear to have been quite intimate. The American government bestowed a decoration upon President Perez Jiménez, the strong-arm President of Venezuela, who has recently joined the company of ex-dictators. In the more remote past, there are other examples of the complacent acceptance by Washington of governments whose moral character one could not possibly approve.

But there is another point of view, frequently expressed by outsiders, and not unknown in the State Department itself. This view maintains that it is dangerous for the United States to identify itself with the forces of reaction, that the consequences of such a course will make more difficult relations with the rising democratic forces in Latin America and will increase hostility to this country. The proponents of this view point to such episodes as the reception accorded to Vice-President Nixon in Caracas as a confirmation of their contention. The wise course may well lie between the two extremes. There are a number of states in Latin America where dictatorial or highly authoritarian rule is likely to exist for some time to come—Paraguay, the Dominican Republic, possibly Nicaragua. We cannot simply wish these governments out of existence. We must remember that genuine democracy, as we conceive it, exists in only a few of the Latin-American states. Costa Rica and Uruguay are almost models. Colombia, despite the troubles of the late forties and early fifties, seems likely to settle down to democratic courses. There are hopeful signs in other republics. But if we apply too austere standards as a condition of friendly intercourse, we will not only make ourselves disliked, but will accomplish little good. On the other hand, we do not need to be offensive in our dealing with dictators or quasi-dictators. Such a course is dangerous.

But what of Communism in Latin America? Is there not here a formidable danger? What steps shall we take to prevent its spread in the New World? How shall we grapple with this question?

First of all, a general word. It is, of course, true that Communism thrives on social and economic inequalities, and that these inequalities exist, often in a gross form, in the states of Latin America. In the second place, it is clear that Communism can and does exploit the sentiment of nationalism and, by capitalizing on the prejudice which exists against the United States, seeks to attain its own ends. In the third place, by emphasizing the success of the Soviet Union in an unprecedented program of industrialization, the Communist propaganda appeals to a widespread feeling in Latin America in favor of broadening the economic base by the diversification of the economy. These are powerful sources of strength.

But there is another side to the question. The establishment of a totalitarian regime does not seem consistent with the mores of the Latin Americans. It requires a different national temperament, a kind of docility that has certainly not been characteristic of the Latin Americans in general. The highly personalized regimes of the Latin-American republics arise—and are overthrown. No one of these republics has ever institutionalized despotism, not even Argentina under Perón. Equally true, no one of these states has ever been disposed to subject the total economy to state control. Indeed, some of the difficulties in which these communities have been plunged have been caused by the failure of the government to exercise sufficient supervision over the economic life of the people. Again, political uniformity would probably be harder to enforce in Latin America than in any other part of the world. An intense individualism is often characteristic of Latin-American party contests. The Communist parties themselves have often been a prey to factionalism. To reduce the population of the most vigorous of these states to slavish obedience to a totalitarian regime will not be easy. There is the influence of the Church. This influence varies from state to state; in many it is not great. But in some of the larger states it is important, and there can be no doubt into which scale that influence will be thrown.

Two other considerations suggest themselves. First, the republics of Latin America are closely geared to the economy of the free world, and in many cases to the economy of the United States. And finally, as in many other instances, the nationalism which express itself so vigorously in these states acts in part as an antidote to any attempted control from Moscow.

But what I have said is, in a sense, theoretical. What has been the policy of the United States with regard

to Communism? It would appear that just after the war
the United States would have liked to see an agreement
among the states of the New World to intervene collec-
tively in the event their institutions were threatened.
It smiled upon and encouraged, perhaps instigated, a
proposal made by Dr. Rodriguez Larreta, the Foreign
Minister of Uruguay, in 1945. " The basic rights of
man," wrote Dr. Larreta at that time, " are part of the
principles of popular government. Thus, though once
exclusively domestic concerns, they now affect international interests and require international protection.
In case of their violation in any American republic, the
community of nations should take collective multi-
lateral action to restore full democracy there." This
view was given " unqualified adherence " by Secretary
James M. Byrnes.

This idea, however, met with a very cool reception
from the majority of the republics. Many of them
distrusted the idea of collective intervention as nothing
less than American intervention in disguise. Their
strong sense of national independence revolted against
any legalization of intermeddling in their affairs. At
the Conference of Bogotá in 1948, the Pan-American
Union was transferred into the Organization of American States. In the charter of the new body it is stated:
" No state or group of states has the right to intervene,

directly or indirectly, for any reason whatever, in the internal or external affairs of any other state. The foregoing principle prohibits not only armed force but also any other form of interference or attempted threat against the personality of the state, or against its political, economic or cultural elements."

On the other hand, the conference showed signs that it was aware of the Communist danger. It adopted a resolution denouncing Communism, and declaring: " It is in accordance with the high common and individual interests of the American republics to meet the special and immediate threat of subversive action of international Communism. Since the said subversive action recognizes no boundaries, the present situation requires adequate internal measures, a high degree of international cooperation looking to eradication of any threat of subversive activity which may endanger democracy and the free way of life in America.

This action was repeated in the Conference of Caracas in 1954, which declared in more emphatic language: " The domination or control of the political institutions of any American state by the international Communist movement, extending to this hemisphere the political system of an extra-Continental power, would constitute a threat to the sovereignty and political independence of the American states, endangering the peace of

America, and would call for a meeting of Consultation to consider the adoption of appropriate action in accordance with existing treaties." These two resolutions lay the basis for common action, and certainly for common consultation in the event of a Communist threat in the New World. It is sometimes said that both the Bogotá and the Caracas resolution were adopted reluctantly and merely to please the United States. It is all the more interesting to analyze the one instance where international Communism established itself in a New World state—that is, in Guatemala.

There can be little question that the government which came into power in Guatemala in 1954 was heavily infiltrated by the Communists. It soon embarked upon a radical program of land distribution, which was speedily perverted to the interests of the Reds. It was, in the spring of 1954, purchasing arms from the Soviet sphere. Its representative at Caracas had spoken out boldly against the resolution introduced by the United States.

In June of 1954 this regime was overthrown by a revolutionary movement originating on the soil of Honduras. The revolutionary leader, Castillo Armas, began his offensive on the 11th of June. On the 23rd, the Arbenz government collapsed.

We are still too near these events to discuss them

with that full knowledge of the facts that the historian desires before making a judgment. Cynics will doubtlessly believe that the revolution was instigated by the United States. There is, however, no evidence to this effect. The most that can be said is that the American government supplied arms to the governments of Honduras and Nicaragua to act as a makeweight against the arms imported into Guatemala. It does not appear that these arms got into the hands of the Guatemalan revolutionaries.

The two most significant facts on which to focus are these. In the first place, there was very little fighting. The Arbenz regime was not defeated in battle; it collapsed. Its collapse suggests that even in this Communist-dominated state, it had not been possible to win the military forces to the side of Communism. On the contrary, Jacopo Arbenz seems to have mediated the creation of a Communist militia simply because he could not depend upon the army, and this may have been one of the major reasons for his downfall.

In the second place, what is interesting is the change in opinion among the Latin-American republics between the Caracas meeting and the events of June. At Caracas, the United States had had its difficulties; Senor Guillermo Toriello had been loudly cheered when he spoke out against the resolution sponsored by the United

States. The states of Latin America had refused to get excited at the menace of the Reds. In June, however, the situation was very different. The call went forth for a meeting of the Organization of American States. There was a widespread feeling of apprehension. Even in Mexico, where President Lázaro Cárdenas had supported the Guatemalan cause, sentiment had shifted toward the United States. Nor did it please the Latin Americans when Guatemala appealed directly to Russia through the Security Council. A vote in that body to consider the Guatemalan appeal was decisively rejected. The Soviet Union was put on notice to keep out of the New World.

All in all, the Guatemalan episode suggests that considerable difficulties would be met if the Communists attempted to take over the government of an American state. Speaking broadly, it seems fair to say that the role of Communism in the states of Latin America has ebbed in the last decade. During the war, when the Communists were stridently supporting the cause of the democracies, they gathered much strength to themselves. But in the years that followed, the shameless dependence of the Communist leaders upon Moscow has become clearer and clearer. Their numbers have been shrinking. In Chile in 1947, the Reds managed to get into the government. They conducted themselves so outrageously that in only a few months President González Vidale got rid of them, and they have never held office again. Moreover, democratic parties of reform have arisen in several of the Latin-American states—the Aprista movement in Peru, the Acción Democrática in Venezuela, the Movimiento Nacional Revolucionario in Bolivia, the Partido Liberación Nacional in Costa Rica. We cannot expect that the policies of these parties will in all cases run parallel with the interests of the United States. But there is much to be said for the view that their relatively moderate character will dilute and perhaps frustrate the Communist menace.

There is one other fact of importance, and an argument of a totally different color, that may serve to justify an optimistic view. The Communist virus has not in general penetrated the military classes in Latin America. These classes are often overconservative. They are, on occasion, concerned with lining their own pockets; but their training, and their connections, does not identify them with the extreme left.

As for the United States, there are some general principles we must cling to. Example is more powerful than precept. The success of popular government in other parts of the world depends in no small degree on how well we make it work in the United States. If we learn to solve our own problems, if we create a better and better society through the medium of the democratic process, if we use the vast wealth we create for the benefit of the mass of men and not for the indulgence of the few, we may be very sure that this fact will have an impact on other countries, not least on those of Latin America.

But there is more to the matter than that. We must learn to distinguish between the measures of social change which are virtually inevitable in these societies, and a lurch into Communism. We must not label every reforming movement " red." We must be patient and forbearing. We ought to be heartened by the experience of Mexico already cited. Mexico went through a phase when silly people thought it was going Bolshevist, though what it was really doing was attempting to create a better social order, sometimes by means that many of us would call ill-advised and that were undoubtedly socialistic in character, but which never suggested a total transformation into an authoritarian society. As time passed the tide of radicalism receded; Mexico returned to the middle of the road; experience proved—perhaps from our prejudiced angle we may say that it was bound to prove—that the socialist answer was an imperfect answer to a very complex problem. If we can forbear hasty action, we may well find that the same lesson can be learned by other Latin-American states. Certainly we shall gain nothing by measures of coercion; we shall only make ourselves disliked the more and diminish our prestige throughout Latin America.

I cannot close this discussion without a general word on the chances of democracy in Latin America. It seems to me obvious that they are very much better than they are, say in the Far East (with the exception of Japan). The *tendency* in Latin America has been towards the growth of orderly popular government. The foundations on which such government rests, wherever it is most successful, are the wide distribution of property and the increase of educational facilities. The history of the larger and more prosperous republics ought to give us hope for the future. The road will not be easy, of course. But the events of the last decade and a half lead to a hopeful rather than a despairing judgment.

Let me turn in my third essay to the critical problem of our economic relations with the states of the South.

LATIN-AMERICAN ECONOMIC RELATIONS WITH THE UNITED STATES

THE STORY OF our economic relations with Latin America cannot fail to have an especial interest for the philosophic historian, for it poses some large questions. In the nineteenth and early twentieth century, the development of the economically retarded sections of the globe was undertaken under one set of conditions; today it is to be undertaken under very different ones. Then, private capital came into these regions, either under the aegis of an imperialist government or, usually, welcomed by the local rulers; embarrassing questions as to the rate of profit were not likely to be asked, and when asked, such was the power of the foreign investor that the proper answer was likely to be forthcoming. At the same time, investors in the capital-exporting countries often subscribed joyfully and sometimes recklessly to issues of bonds floated by the undeveloped states, and the process of internal development was assisted by the ease with which such loans were marketed. Today, the situation is somewhat different. Private capital still plays a large—even a predominant —part in the picture. It can no longer count on military force to protect it, and in some instances it is likely to find that the public sentiment of the capital-receiving state demands not only a share of the profits, but also a share of the management. As for loans to governments, the private loan seems to be going out of fashion; and it is by public agencies to a large, though not to an exclusive, degree that the funds are provided, in part, for the further development of the undeveloped countries through borrowing. These conditions suggest a philosophic question of great import —the question as to whether a way will be found to encourage the importation of capital and the assistance of the entrepreneurs from the great industrial nations in sufficient measure to stimulate the economic growth of the less mature countries of the world on a scale to meet their social aspirations. It is not for the historian to answer this question. What he can do is tell a little of the story of the past and analyze conditions as he finds them today.

Before embarking upon that study in relation to Latin America, however, something must be said, not of investment but of trade, of the significance of that trade, and of the problems to which it gives rise. Our *export* trade with Latin America got off to a good start in the 1820's and 30's, but it rarely exceeded 10 per cent of our total exports from that time forward until the end of the century. It increased only a little in the years from 1901–10, being then about 11.7 per cent; and it was only 12.4 per cent in the years 1911–15. Since then, the figures—stated for five year periods—are as follows: 1915–20, 19.7 per cent; 1921–25, 17 per cent; 1926–30, 17.9 per cent; 1931–35, 15 per cent; 1936–40, 19 per cent; 1941–45 (the war years) 15 per cent; 1946–50, 26 per cent; 1951–55, 28.8 per cent; 1957, the last year for which accurate statistics are available, 28.8 per cent. It will be observed that there has been a very striking gain since World War II, and that Latin-American trade bulks very large indeed in our foreign commerce. These figures are the more striking if we compare them with our sales to Asia, which have rarely risen above 14 per cent, and almost never above 20 per cent. Looking at them one wonders why in the minds of many Americans the Orient has been an object of such special solicitude from the angle of our foreign commerce. Our *imports* from Latin America show considerable variation, in the quinquennium of 1876–80, for example, they rose to 30 per cent of the total; they were 36 per cent in the years 1915–20; but the normal figure down to the First World War was in the neighborhood of 20 per cent. Since the war the totals, in quinquennia, are are follows: 1921–25, 28 per cent; 1926–30, 25 per cent; 1931–35, 24.6 per cent; 1936–40, 23.4 per cent; 1941–45, 40 per cent; 1946–50, 37 per cent; 1951–55, 30 per cent, and in 1957, 32.5 per cent. Here again the comparison with Asia is illuminating, especially in the period since the Second World War. Imports from Asia were less than 19 per cent in the years 1946–50, less than 17 per cent in the years 1951–55, and less than 16 per cent in 1957. We might look too, for a moment, at our trade with Europe. In the first decade of the twentieth century 70 per cent of our exports and over 50 per cent of our imports were sent to or received from that continent. Today the percentages are in the neighborhood of 25 per cent. We need no further evidence to underline the high significance of our trade with our " southern neighbors."

The figures, however, may be viewed from another angle. The striking fact is that for many of the Latin-American republics, the principal market and the principal supplier is the United States. Thus, Mexico in 1958 took 73 per cent of its imports from this country and exported 78 per cent of its products to us. For Cuba the figures were 65 per cent and 75 per cent. In the Caribbean area as a whole, the United States is, in almost every case, the first supplier and the best customer. For the continent of South America, the figures are not so striking. Countries like Argentina and Uruguay are not oriented toward the " colossus of the North." But, on the basis of recent figures, Brazil buys half of what it imports in the American market, and Colombia, 71 per cent. The existence of this trade relationship may be a source of strength, or a source of weakness; dependence on a given market may produce irritation, but it may and should underline the necessity of maintaining good relations. The very volume of the trade almost inevitably suggests a closer political relationship, and does something to explain why the Pan-American idea has shown such remarkable vitality, despite the differences which exist with regard to political institutions.

There is another point to be made. The trade with Latin America, so far as imports are concerned, is a trade in raw materials. Latin America was and is our principal foreign supplier of important products, of sugar (most of which comes from Cuba, of course), of coffee (the greater part of which crop comes from Brazil and Colombia), and of bananas (which come from the Caribbean area and Ecuador). The prices of these raw materials have, as an historical matter, fluctuated wildly. Sugar, for example, after the First World War, soared to unprecedented heights; the price in

New York, f. o. b., on May 1920 was 22½ cents and then after a speculative orgy, it plunged down to about 3¼ cents in December. Coffee has had a similar history. The control of the market is the more difficult, since no one country in Latin America is in control of all of the crop; and an element of instability is introduced into our relations with our suppliers, which is sometimes the cause of bitterness and recrimination. One has only to recall the plaints of American householders, and the retorts of the Brazilians, a few years ago when coffee went above a dollar a pound.

There have been attempts to stabilize both coffee and sugar prices by international understanding. The United States was a party to the Inter-American Coffee Agreement during the Second World War. The agreement was signed by fourteen coffee-producing countries and the United States. Under its terms, quotas were established governing both the export and import of the product; there can be little doubt that it prevented a runaway market. There was, however, a good deal of grumbling on both sides. Coffee doubled in price under the agreement, not wholly to the satisfaction of the American consumers, while the Latin Americans complained of inadequate profits. The agreement itself broke down in 1948. The reserves accumulated under the plan were exhausted, and coffee nearly doubled in price in 1949. At the present time a new agreement is in effect, but the United States is not a party to it.

With regard to sugar, the first attempt at price regulation, the so-called Chadbourne plan, made in 1931, soon broke down. The second, in 1937, ran afoul of difficulties with the advent of the Second World War. Since then, two other agreements have been negotiated, one in 1953 and another in 1958. There has not been since 1953 a runaway market in sugar, though prices breached the limits set by the agreement of 1953. Perhaps the safest thing that can be said with regard to the regulation of sugar prices is that the interest in international action has remained and that, whatever the limitations of procedure, the worse excesses of a free market have been eliminated.

What is the position of the United States with regard to projects of this kind? As I have already said, the American government was a partner to the Inter-American Coffee Agreement of 1940. Its position with regard to price stabilization today is best expressed in the report of Milton Eisenhower, the President's brother, rendered after a visit to Central America and Panama in 1959.

Alluding to the agreement with regard to coffee mentioned above, Dr. Eisenhower takes a rather cautious view. " I recommend," he says, " that the United States, if requested to do so, cooperate to the extent of furnishing such information as laws and regulations permit, to assist the producing countries in enforcing agreement among marketing quotas. I do not believe that we should go beyond this." Then follows a word of warning. After a melancholy—a justifiably melancholy —discussion of our own difficulties with agricultural prices, Dr. Eisenhower goes on: " This experience, involving one nation, suggests the difficulty of having stabilization programs succeed when many nations are involved. It should be a pointed warning to the producing nations not to place too great faith on marketing quotas for coffee. If such quotas do for a time stabilize the price of coffee at a fairly good level, this in itself would stimulate further production, cause the accumulation of additional surpluses, and lead to the collapse of world coffee prices." Whether this gloomy view is sound economics, I leave to the professionals in the field. But a similar judgment is expressed by Vladimir P. Timoshenko and Bons C. Swerling in their very careful study, *The World's Sugar*. Speaking of the agreement of 1953, they say: " It accepts as its main objective the reconciliation of essentially irreconcilable national sugar policies, while failing to come to grips with identifiable underlying difficulties. While it would be dangerous to generalize too confidently with regard to agreements of this type, it is certainly the case that they are exposed to all sorts of dangers arising out of the shifting political and diplomatic scene."

But let us turn from the question of trade to the question of investment. The traditional method of economic growth for the less advanced countries has, until recently, been the importation of foreign capital; and in this regard Latin America was no exception to the rule. Most of the early capital was British, but the United States got into the game earlier than some people suppose. The epic story of Commodore Vanderbilt and the Panama railroad is a case in point. Most of the American capital, however, down to 1890 went either to Cuba or to Mexico, principally to the latter. Professor J. Fred Rippy estimates that by 1897 the total American investment had reached about $320,000,000, of which the greater part in Mexico was in railways and mines, and in Cuba in sugar. In the same period, too, was developed the banana business, and in 1899, just at the close of the century, the United Fruit Company was incorporated. Since we are dealing with one of the most typical examples of what hostile critics describe as economic imperialism, we may examine this development in a little more detail, especially in reference to Central America. It was Minor C. Keith who, in 1884, having secured a contract to build a railroad line across the little republic of Costa Rica, took up the cultivation of bananas as a way to make his project pay off. Thus began a development which spread through Central America, embracing Guatemala and Honduras as well as Costa Rica, and eventually extending to other areas, such as Colombia, Panama, and very recently, Ecuador. There is no question that the original grants made to the capitalists who entered this new business were much more generous than accords with the temper of today. The risks were great and the rewards high. There is no question, either, that the banana interests often exercised a powerful influence in the politics of the region. There seems to be at least one case in which the president of an important American company stimulated a revolution in one of the Latin American states and received as his reward a very fine contract indeed.

It has been easy for those who raise the cry of economic imperialism to point to this episode, and to the United Fruit Company, in terms of deprecation. For this very reason I should like to analyze this whole matter of "economic imperialism" and see where a rational consideration of the subjects brings us out. We have a perspective on the matter today that ought to be useful.

Let us first state as strongly as possible the case against these great aggregations of capital, as it is often felt by Latin Americans. In the first place, the very size of some of these companies is itself a source of distrust and is thought of as a threat to the independence of the state itself. The wealth and power of United Fruit is greater than that of government itself in some parts of Central America. It is not strange that such a situation begets difficulties. Moreover, Latin Americans have a long memory. They know that the early concessions to American capital, however justified by the mores of the times and by the need to provide great incentives to match great risks, were from the present angle of vision often excessive. They know that there were occasions when the great fruit companies, by their political intrigues, kept some parts of Central America in turmoil. They know that in the past venality and undue influence have played a part in the economic development of their countries. They feel that the great foreign corporations are not very likely to be sympathetic with projects of social reform, unless indeed, these projects are of their own initiative; and, rightly or wrongly, they attribute to the growth of these companies, a tendency towards what has come to be regarded as an evil, namely, a " monocultural " economy.

But there is a strong case on the other side, and looking at the matter objectively, one comes to the conclusion that the migration of American capital to Latin America ought most emphatically to be in the interest of the Latin Americans themselves, and can continue to be, with wisdom and restraint on both sides.

In the first place, it is difficult to see how any substantial development could have taken place in the banana business without the foreign enterpriser. The countries of the Caribbean area were not in a position to undertake the large-scale investments involved. The capital simply was not there.

In the second place, contrary to a view often held, the greater part of the funds used in these enterprises are not siphoned off to the United States, but remain in the country itself. A recent study of the activities of United Fruit makes this clear. In the year 1954–55, the amount received in six banana producing countries was in the neighborhood of 160 million dollars. Of this sum, 56 million was paid out in wages; 18 million more went in local taxes; 27 million was expended in local purchases; and 35 million was spent on imported goods and equipment. Only 17.8 million was remitted abroad for dividends. No doubt the figures for a single year ought not to be regarded as typical, and if one looks at the calculations for the individual states there are wide variations; but the fact remains that a very large proportion of the sums received by the Company for its products are spent within the countries concerned. The notion that what takes place is a drain of the natural wealth of the community is far from the truth.

There are other factors which ought to be taken into account. The level of wages paid by United Fruit and its rivals in the Caribbean area is undeniably higher than that which is paid to most native workers. It is true that part of the labor used is imported; but even so, it is obvious that whatever is paid out in wages tends towards a more prosperous economy. In addition, workers for the American companies enjoy many advantages. They are better housed, on the whole; they are provided with better care from the point of view of public health; they are provided with company schools; in many instances they can buy at company stores at a rate lower than that fixed by local merchants. These circumstances, it is true, have not exempted the Company from labor disturbances; but the facts are as stated. In addition, United Fruit has established a Pan-American Agricultural School at Zamorano in Honduras, where young men coming from many different countries receive practical instruction in agriculture. None of the graduates is allowed to enter the employ of the company itself.

It is sometimes said that the fruit companies engross

the best lands in the countries in which they operate. Yet the proportion of crop lands used for the cultivation of bananas is small in every one of the states where banana culture is common—as little as 1 per cent in Guatemala, 7 per cent in Costa Rica, and 12 per cent in Ecuador, where the figure is highest. Land-hunger is not a fundamental problem in any of these countries as matters stand today. Whether it will become so in the long future is a question which we need not examine.

But we have not reached the end of the argument with regard to what is described as " economic imperialism." The crux of the question is this. It lies with the state which receives foreign capital to regulate the conditions under which it operates, and to see to it that the social interest of the total community is well served and protected. After all, the state is sovereign; it can prescribe the terms on which a private corporation operates; it can tax, within the limits of prudence; or perhaps, if it wishes, beyond the limits of prudence; and it and its agents are rightly chargeable with responsibility for failure to do what needs to be done. It is fair to say that in our own time the reckless surrender of the public interest to outsiders is no longer characteristic of Latin-American governments. But, says the denouncer of " economic imperialism," cannot the

American investor call the great government of the United States to his aid? Cannot the government of the capital-receiving state be overawed? To answer this question, we must first note that the United States is bound by two solemn protocols to abstain from intervention in the affairs of the Latin-American republics; resort to armed force, or the threat of armed force, is therefore banned. The State Department can make representations, of course, but is not usually in a position to go much further. And the actual policies of the United States have certainly not been unduly protective of the interests of American capital. I shall return to this point later.

I have dealt with the investment in bananas at some length because it represents one of the early forms of export capital, and because it points up some general principles that it is well for us to bear in mind. Let me now say a word about a second crop which deeply engages the interest of the United States, and which also has a fairly long history. That crop is sugar.

The center of the sugar industry in the New World, as we all know, is Cuba. There were substantial investments there in the colonial period, and it is a fair question to raise as to whether the sugar people played an important part in the stimulus of hostility to Spain, which resulted in the war of 1898. It is, however, not easy to answer categorically. Professor J. W. Pratt, who has examined this question, has shown that there was some pressure brought on the McKinley administration to take action to put an end to the insurrection in Cuba, though American intervention was not explicitly demanded. He has also shown that at least one important American sugar planter was firmly opposed to war. None of this, as he himself says, is conclusive. But it seems right to say of the conflict with Spain that it owed its origin to a widespread public mood, rather than to any special interest, and that this mood was expressed in every part of the country without much regard to the economic interests involved.

In another sense, however, there was undeniably a connection between the war of 1898 and American economic policy. The Cuban question was then, and has been since, one of the most interesting illustrations of the disastrous effects that our tariff legislation may have on another economy. By the McKinley Act of 1890 sugar was put on the free list, and the natural result was a substantial increase in Cuban sugar production; by the ill-fated Wilson bill of 1894 it was again subjected to a duty; and this reversal of policy was a factor in bringing about an economic recession in the island, also in preparing the way for the revolution of 1895. Nor is this the only instance in which we have dealt a body blow to the Cuban economy. A still worse case was the passage of the Hawley-Smoot Act in 1930. There never was a piece of protective tariff legislation more thoroughly unjustified; economists were almost unanimously opposed to it; yet the President signed it, and the result was a severe drop in the price of sugar on the Cuban market, and a series of political troubles that lasted until the situation became more stable with the adoption of new legislation in 1934. The point that is to be made here has a more general application. In an economy of such vast proportions as that of the United States, changes in the tariff may well have a limited effect; but they are a serious matter for our Latin-American friends. Only recently the raising of the zinc and lead rates has affronted our friends in Peru, and a rise in the copper tariff may work serious damage to the economy of Chile.

While we are discussing the tariff, we should look for a moment at the situation with regard to Cuba during the last quarter of a century. Since the Jones-Costigan Act of 1934, Cuban sugar has been admitted into the United States under a quota system. Since the American sugar industry is subsidized, this amounts to giving the Cuban sugar growers a higher price than the world price in the American market. Since, even after a quarter of a century of effort to diversify the Cuban economy, by far the greater proportion of Cuban exports is in sugar, this means that there is a very close connection between the Cuban economy and our own. Just how vital this connection is, one cannot say. Cuba is a low-cost producer, and under free-market conditions probably has an advantage greater than that of any other country in the world market. But the sale of sugar is controlled by an international agreement, and it is therefore by no means certain that if the United States restricted or limited its takings of Cuban sugar, the loss could be at once made up elsewhere. I venture no prediction on this matter.

We have dealt with two of the great staples which connect the United States with Latin America. We should say something about oil, which, like bananas and sugar, has a relatively long history in connection with our " southern neighbors." The first important exploitations of oil in a Latin-American country were, of course, undertaken in Mexico. The first gushers came in as early as 1901; by 1910 production equalled 14 million barrels; by 1920 Mexican oil production exceeded the production of all oil fields in the world outside the United States. These can be little question that American oil interests contributed to the support of the Constitutionalist forces under General Venustiano Carranza in the revolutionary struggles of the second decade; and it would appear that at the same time they organized a private force to protect their holdings from the evils of war. But the outcome of the revolution was hardly to their taste; the Constitution of 1917 declared that the title to all minerals in the subsoil was in the state; and in the course of the twenties and thirties the American oil companies were hard put to it to maintain their position. It is not necessary to trace the controversy in detail, but in 1938 the administrations of General Lázaro Cárdenas nationalized the oil industry, and it is still under government operation at the present day. What, in these circumstances, was the position of the United States? Our government certainly behaved with great moderation. It naturally pressed for compensation for American owners; but the sum finally fixed was modest indeed. Throughout the two decades when the oil controversy was simmering, the temptation to intervene directly was steadily put aside; indeed, American public sentiment was at all times opposed to any such step.

The policies of the Mexican government were naturally shocking to stout conservatives. So, too, was similar action by the Bolivian government in 1937. Were not these examples likely to be followed? Would they not open the door to similar action in other parts of Latin America? After twenty years we are in a position to give at least a partial answer to that question in the negative.

One reason for this is that the experience of the Mexican government with nationalized oil has not been a particularly happy one. In the first years of nationalization, the authorities had to fight a constant battle with the workers, who demanded higher wages and more benefits than the traffic would bear. After 1946 the industry came under the direction of a highly capable man, Antonio Bermúdez. Yet Mexican production has never approached even half the figure that it reached in 1921; the number of new wells drilled is a fraction of what it was at the height of the oil boom; Mexico has been an importer, not an exporter, of refined oil. Even after efficient operation had succeeded the wrangling of the early years, the case for imitation was by no means convincing.

The question of oil production has, however, arisen in connection with not a few other Latin-American states. The sensational development of the Venezuelan oil industry is well known, and today Venezuela is the third largest producer in the world, being exceeded only by the United States and the Soviet Union. There, the industry is in private hands, but the government shares generously in the operation and has recently asked and received even more generous consideration.

It is not too much to say that the Venezuelan economy has thrived on oil. Peru has also relied upon private capital for the most part in the development of the industry. So, too, has Ecuador, though in this case production is very small. Colombia, after a flirtation with the idea of government operation, abandoned the idea.

There are, however, standouts among the Latin-American governments. In Brazil the oil question is a hot political issue, and the wells are under government operation. Argentina has also tried government operation; indeed, it pioneered in this field even before the oil discoveries in Mexico. In Chile the same thing is true. But it is significant that in none of these countries has the industry reached any very great successes. In all of them production is meager, by the comparative standard—only 3,000,000 barrels in Brazil and Chile, 31,000,000 in Argentina. Moreover, in the last-named state, the present government has resorted to a new policy by which private companies have been given a stake in the drilling of new wells and in the development of the industry.

One may speculate with caution about the future. To an observer of world trends, it would appear that the notion that nationalization of industry is the answer to the woes of society seems distinctly on the decline.

This is certainly the case in Europe, where the old socialist doctrines have been more and more losing their appeal. Save for the current case of Cuba, may not the same thing be true in Latin America?

It is not possible, of course, to survey all the aspects of the migration of investment capital to Latin America. There has been a substantial mining investment, of which two prime examples are investment in copper in Chile and, very recently, in iron in Venezuela. More than a fifth of the total exportations of capital have by now been in the field of manufactures, and in Mexico and Cuba very substantial sums have gone into public utilities. Diversification is substantial. And if the total figures be scanned, they will show that of the total American investments abroad, 33 per cent are today in Latin America. These figures, however, are not entirely encouraging. For comparatively, the rate of growth has been less impressive than in some other areas. Canada has been the great receiver of capital in the last decade. In Western Europe there has been a doubling of American investment since 1950. The relative increase in these other areas suggests problems which we must analyze in the course of this discussion.

For the moment, however, let us turn to another aspect of the economic relations of the United States with Latin America, that is, the field of public lending—

the floating of Latin-American loans in the American market. In the nineteenth century very, very little activity was observable in this field. The world money market up to the First World War was in London. The American public had bought substantial quantities of Mexican and Cuban bonds, and it had also invested in the securities of countries such as Haiti and the Dominican Republic, in which American marines offered some guarantee of payment of interest and reimbursement of principal. But beyond this, little had been done. With the period of the twenties, a different picture presents itself, and one that reflects little credit on the American capacity to act as the world's banker. A brief reading of the history of the nineteenth century might have unfolded a grisly story with regard to Latin-American securities of the epoch. An elementary understanding of the foreign trade problem would have revealed the fact that there were large risks involved. A study of our tariff policies would have contributed to a cautious view of international moneylending. A wider judgment of the situation from the vantage point of Washington would have pointed up some of the perils involved in the flotation of foreign bonds. A deeper sense of responsibility on the part of investment bankers themselves might have saved American investors from more than one act of folly. None of these elements entered into the problem. In these years of prosperity and of general acceptance of a largely laissez-faire philosophy, it was possible to market the bonds of many Latin-American states without any careful examination of the future on the part of sellers and buyers alike. Between 1920 and 1930, nearly two billion dollars worth of Latin-American securities were sold on the American market. Over a billion dollars worth were the bonds of Argentina, Brazil, and Chile; Colombia and Peru account for another 300 million; and such a state as Bolivia—with anything but a good credit record—got 68 million. Apparently what was good for the bankers who marketed the bonds was thought to be good for the investors who bought them.

As to what was good for the bankers, there can be little argument. It is not easy to pass judgment on the terms of the individual loans, but the spread between the price the banking houses paid for the bonds and the price the public paid for them in many cases represented a handsome profit. Nor was the business carried on without some evidences of shady finance. The son of the President of Peru got a large fee for his " services " in connection with a Peruvian loan. " Finder's fees," as they were poetically called, were common. One small banking house, which floated a loan for El Salvador, got a spread of more than 11 points on the transaction, and was able to give $120,000 to one individual for his assistance in facilitating the loan. The story has been told in more detail by Professor Rippy in his admirable work, *Globe and Hemisphere*, and in still more complete fashion in the Hearings of the Senate Committee on Finance of the Seventy-Second Congress.

What was the result? With the advent of the world depression, service on the greater part of the issues was suspended. As commodity prices fell, it was more and more difficult for many of the Latin-American countries to find the dollars in which to remit their interest payments. Confronted with all kinds of difficulties at home, it is not strange that they thought first of the needs of their own people, and last of the obligations due to foreigners, all the more so because of the atmosphere which surrounded many of the flotations themselves. By 1934, out of the total issues then amounting to about a billion and a half, over a billion one hundred thousand were in default. Only the Dominican Republic and Haiti, still under American customs control, were meeting their obligations in full. In the case of Chile and Colombia, Costa Rica, Guatemala, and Uruguay, the default on interest was total. In the case of Brazil it was almost total. It did not add to the good cheer of the bond holders when the Chilean government took advantage of the fall in the price of its securities to buy them up on the open market, and thus reduce its indebtedness, while failing on its interest payments.

It is worthwhile to follow further the story of the Latin-American bond issues, if only to add a somewhat more cheerful note to the story. The government of the United States was reluctant to put severe pressure on the debtor states at a time when the good-neighbor policy was being developed so prosperously. Responsibility for meeting the problems of the bondholders was in the hands of a body known as the Foreign Bondholders Protective Council, and in the quarter of a century since 1934 this body has done something to retrieve the situation by negotiations carried on with the debtor governments. By 1945 less than 50 per cent of the Latin-American bonds were in total default as to interest, with a par value of something like a billion; by 1948 there had been a further shrinkage; by 1957, of Latin-American bonds outstanding, 11.3 per cent were in complete default, 87.3 per cent were being served on an adjusted basis, and only 1.4 per cent were being served in full. Of those on an adjusted basis the adjustment—downwards—was often a very substantial one.

Yet the need of the countries to the south for public

funds remains. In the period since the end of the Second World War the same questions have arisen that arose in the twenties. How is the development of these vast regions to take place without some borrowing abroad? How are the aspirations of these peoples for a better life to be met if they are not accorded financial assistance? This is one of the key problems of the era in which we are living.

Before describing what has been done and what is proposed, a word should be said about the idea of a South American Marshall plan. This is one of those thoughts that has an alluring sound, but which becomes less attractive when subjected to a more exact analysis. For the Marshall plan, the most brilliant financial operation in the field of American diplomacy, was carried out under conditions vitally different from those that obtain with regard to Latin America. In the first place, we were acting under very important pressures. Europe, in misery at the end of the war, was a possible prize of the first order for the Soviet Union. A Communist take-over of this region would have been nothing less than a disaster. Here lay the region of the most advanced technology in the world. Here lay the region which we had rescued from the poison of Hitlerism with the blood of our soldiers. Here lay the region which Americans knew best. It is not strange that it was here that we were ready to make the greatest effort and to pursue the boldest politics. But there was more to the matter than that. The Marshall plan involved certain definite actions on the part of the European participating nations. It meant the cooperation of these nations with one another in the building of their own economies, a kind of informal economic association far from union, but a long way from individual action. It meant a pledge from these nations that they would put their own economic houses in order. It meant still further that they would set aside in what were called counterpart funds a considerable amount in their own currencies to be devoted to the work of reconstruction. All these things were of the essence in the evolution and in the success of the Marshall plan.

There is another collateral point to be made about the Marshall plan. While a very large proportion of the funds made available to European governments were spent in the United States, a not inconsiderable sum was devoted to offshore payments, many of these payments in Latin America. The gain to the republics to the south was therefore substantial and ought not to be forgotten.

Of the conditions which produced the Marshall plan some may be reproduced in the future. One would like to think that the day will come when the Latin-

American states will be able to act together to a greater degree than has hitherto been possible. One would like to think that they would pursue fiscal policies that would facilitate economic aid. But *one* of the conditions which was present in 1947 and 1948 is not likely to occur in the same guise again. The sense of urgency generated by Soviet aggression has diminished. Whether today the Kremlin is in good faith seeking a more moderate policy or whether it is merely laying " springs to catch wood-cocks " is, in a sense, beyond the point. The climate of 1960 is essentially different from the climate of 1948.

In dealing with the question of our postwar policy towards Latin America, we must see it from two angles of vision. We must ask ourselves to what degree and in what way private capital can assist in the development. Loans, of the type of the 1920's, are of course out of the question. Indeed, the market for Latin-American bonds is nonexistent at the present time. Nonetheless, the way is open for substantial assistance along this line through public lending agencies created during and after the war.

The first of these agencies is the Export-Import Bank, established by act of Congress in 1934. Fundamentally, the Bank was created in order to stimulate the exports of the United States. It is still the case that its loans must be used for the purchase of commodities in this country. But this by no means implies that these loans are granted only with the interests of the American exporter in mind. A very large part of them are directly related to the economic development of the receiving nation, for the protection of its exchange, for economic reconstruction, for the building of industrial plants or of electric power plants, to mention only a few objectives. In 1950, to further illustrate, the Bank extended a credit of 150 million dollars to the Mexican government for the joint construction with the United States of a dam on the Rio Grande. Steel plants in Brazil and Chile have been financed. One hundred million was lent to Peru for the development of its copper resources. Railway development, electric power, and agricultural growth have all been among the purposes served by the lending institution. The rates of interest have been higher by about 2 per cent than the rate of United States Government securities, but they certainly have not been extortionate and, considering the credit standing of many of the Latin-American republics, can hardly be considered unreasonable.

The Export-Import Bank, it will be understood, makes loans to governments and sometimes to private firms in all parts of the world. At the end of 1956 it had authorized credits of about eight billion three hundred thousand dollars, of which nearly three billion had been extended to the Latin-American states. In 1957 the Export-Import Bank authorized credits of $290,161,000 to Latin-American states and in 1958 the amount of credits was a total of $478,900,000. Every one of these states had gotten something, the sums varying from less than two million to El Salvador to one billion one hundred and fifty-five million to Brazil. The principal beneficiaries besides Brazil were Argentina and Mexico.

In addition to the Export-Import Bank, there is also the International Bank for Reconstruction and Development, in which the United States is the largest stockholder. This institution, of course, is not subject to the restrictions imposed upon the American institution, in that the funds which it lends can be spent anywhere in the world. It has done a substantial business in loans to Latin America since its establishment in 1945. In January, 1959, the outstanding loans to Latin-American states amounted to about eight hundred million dollars. The rate of lending was in the neighborhood of one hundred and fifty million a year.

There are, however, still other agencies which ought to be mentioned in connection with the meeting of Latin-American credit needs. There is, for example, the Development Loan Fund, placed under the aegis of the International Cooperation Administration subject to fewer restrictions than those imposed on the Export-Import Bank, and authorized to make loans that can be repaid in the local currency instead of in dollars. This fund has only recently been established, and as yet only small grants have been made to Latin-American states. We cannot yet judge of its usefulness.

Finally, Congress includes in the foreign aid bill each year funds for technical assistance (the outgrowth of President Truman's Point Four), and also permits investment guarantees to be given on a limited scale to private corporations investing in Latin America.

Despite this array of agencies, the complaints of inadequate credit resources still resound. After his mission to Central America in 1958, Dr. Milton Eisenhower suggested the establishment of an Inter-American Development Bank. This Bank, created in 1959, is authorized to make soft loans to a limited degree. The usefulness of such a bank remains to be measured.

How shall we judge, in broader terms, the central problem of Latin-American borrowing? The first thing to be observed is that the private market for Latin-American securities seems to have pretty well dried up. The experience of the thirties has militated against the flotation of new loans in the New York market. There seems little prospect that the situation will change. The needs of our southern neighbors will undoubtedly have to be met by the public agencies that we have enumerated. Are these agencies adequate? The question is not easily answered. In any case, the development of the Latin-American countries will not and cannot be wholly a matter of public lending. The greater role in that development is likely to be through private investment, as it has been in the past. Eighty per cent of the funds expended in Latin America have come from private sources.

The course of private investment obviously does not depend upon the policies of the government of the United States. It depends upon the policies of the capital-receiving countries. It is obviously not possible to apply the same standards to all of them. They vary in the degree of political stability which they enjoy; they vary in their hospitality to foreign capital; they vary in the quality of their labor. All one can say is that, without reasonably favorable conditions, development is likely to be slow. The extraordinary recovery that has taken place in Europe during the last decade has given that continent a new attractiveness in the eyes of American enterprise. Canada exercises a constant charm as a field for new investment. So, too, in increasing degree do Australia and New Zealand. The position of Latin America in comparison is perhaps less favorable than it was a decade ago. But, on the other hand, as compared with many other parts of the world, Latin America enjoys a comparative advantage. The Middle East is a region in constant turmoil, and the great oil investments of American companies are jeopardized, not only by the political instability of the area, but by the discovery of new sources of supply in the Sahara and Libya. Africa, or a large part of it, is passing through the birth pangs of a new era, and one can hardly hope for untroubled advance. Countries like India, in the Far East, are so poor as to offer no very inviting field to the American entrepreneur. Furthermore, to state the matter positively, if one views the matter broadly, the trend in the greater states of Latin America seems towards more political stability. It rests, of course, with the people of these states whether this trend will be continued.

What is true with regard to political conditions is, in the broad sense, true with regard to governmental economic policies. The dogma that nationalized industry is a reasonable and desirable social goal has been badly shaken in the last decade. It has been more and more widely rejected in Europe. It seems to be weakening in the principal Latin-American countries. Mexico affords the best examples of the new trends. But the policies of some of the other larger countries point in the same direction.

There is another reason why, always excepting Europe and Canada, Latin America is a hopeful area for the American entrepreneur. The great key industries are in the larger and more stable states, being supplemented by manufactures of another kind, which minister to the needs of the growing middle class, and by the growth of the distributive industries. The success of Sears Roebuck in Mexico City is an example of a type of investment that might in time become more and more common. There is a broader basis for the development and exploitation of the varied human needs in this part of the world than can be true for a long time in the Middle East, in most of Asia, or in most of Africa.

Of course the more hopeful elements in the situation can be vitiated by unwise governmental policies. Restrictions on the transfer of profits to the United States, no matter what the motive, inevitably exercise a chilling effect upon investment. Very heavy taxes can quench the spirit of enterprise. A labor movement that makes unduly onerous demands on the entrepreneur can do much damage. But the one thing that ought to be emphasized is that there seem solid grounds for believing that the general climate is improving; and by the comparative standard Latin America ought to be capable of very substantial economic development in the next half century.

Finally, much depends upon the conduct of the American economy and upon the attitude which we take towards our " southern neighbors." It is almost impossible to overemphasize the importance of this point. It is always difficult for us really to catch up with the present. Man lives in the past, often in the remote past. But it is possible that one of the most revolutionary changes that has taken place in the Western world since the end of World War II is the increasing skill which the economies of the great states are now being managed. We are not yet in a position to throw up our hats, and proclaim that the worse excesses of the business cycle have been prevented for all time. But we can say with some definiteness that much progress has been made in promoting financial stability. Such stability inevitably affects the political climate; it promotes the growth of that middle class on which, as I have before stated, democratic government depends; and while it would be wrong to say that inflation prevents the importation of capital (Brazil seems to refute such a generalization), the foreign enterpriser would prefer in most cases to do business in a country in whose currency he has faith. I need hardly add that stability is almost a *sine qua non* for large-scale borrowing.

Judging from the events of the last decade and a half, the governments of Latin America have been coming to recognize this salient fact. Most of them are managing their finances with prudence at the present time. Argentina is making a sensational comeback, after an era of widespread inflation. Chile is mastering its difficulties. Colombia is doing better than ever before. Even such a state as Bolivia, which has passed through a period of wild currency inflation, is today moving towards stability. As these words are written, only Brazil, of the larger countries, has not yet succeeding in controlling its financial situation.

In this closing essay, I shall sum up the generalizations that flow from what I have already said, and add a few words to reinforce the main points. Let me say again that in the various areas of the world, Latin America ought to hold a special place in the thought of Americans. Admittedly, it is not as important as Europe. The political and economic health of the Western world is vitally tied up with the economic and social progress of the great nations across the seas. Europe is in the midst of an enormous boom, which strengthens all of us. Admittedly, too, Canada is of great importance. The possibilities of development are enormous. But once we have made these exceptions, no region is more significant than Latin America. Physically, it is safer from direct attack than any other area. For many reasons, it is less likely to fall a victim to subversion than is the Near East or some of the countries of Asia. Its population is, whatever its racial mixture, tied by its culture to the nations of the West. The Latin American temperament, with its vigorous strain in individualism, sometimes riotous individualism, is less well adapted to the Communist philosophy than that of some of the countries of the Far East. The forces that make for democracy are stronger in many of the Latin American countries than they can possibly be, say in the Arab lands, or in such a country as Indonesia, or in the newborn republics of Africa. The degree of economic sophistication which exists in these countries is certainly greater than that which exists in any of the countries I have mentioned. The ancient heritage of anti-colonial prejudice, which is present in Africa and in Asia is weaker, though still existent, in the republics of the South. The economic ties which bind these countries to the West are stronger than in most other parts of the world. Taking all these facts into account, it seems clear that the future of Latin America is a matter of vast moment to the United States, and that we cannot afford to allow our foreign policy to be diverted from this region. On the contrary, we need to step up our interest in it. On that larger horizon which ought to animate every American to renewed effort on the international scale, Latin America looms large, and will loom larger tomorrow.